Y0-BEC-940

Archaeology

Archaeology

Discovering the World's Secrets

Gaynor Aaltonen

This book is dedicated to Isobel

Author's Acknowledgements

With thanks to all who contributed, but a special word of thanks in no particular order to William Aaltonen, Vanessa Daubney, John Turing and Charles T. G. Clarke.

This edition published in 2021 by Arcturus Publishing Limited
26/27 Bickels Yard, 151–153 Bermondsey Street,
London SE1 3HA

Copyright © Arcturus Holdings Limited

All rights reserved. No part of this publication may be reproduced, stored in a retrieval system, or transmitted, in any form or by any means, electronic, mechanical, photocopying, recording or otherwise, without prior written permission in accordance with the provisions of the Copyright Act 1956 (as amended). Any person or persons who do any unauthorised act in relation to this publication may be liable to criminal prosecution and civil claims for damages.

AD007172UK

Printed in the UK

CONTENTS

Introduction

"Order is Heaven's first law"

Alexander Pope

Archaeology opens windows into the past. It allows us to wonder at the riches of Tutankhamun's tomb, feel the pathos of the medieval serf scratching a living from feudal soil and marvel at the sublime cave art of the hunter-gatherer. From its beginnings, archaeology has challenged established views by ordering, analysing and rigorously re-ordering the evidence of the past, transforming our view of the ancient world. Piece by painstaking piece, it has helped us to reconstruct and understand human life, and rewrite the history of *Homo sapiens*.

Archaeology in the 21st century is a rigorous and demanding discipline. Trying to decipher the human past requires a broad range of skills, framed by scientific methods. The sense of mystery and the drama of an important find are still there, but they go hand in hand with methodical scholarship and sheer hard work. Huge advances in science are helping us to find, understand and reinterpret the past, which has plenty to say about subjects that have resonance for today's world, such as climate change. Archaeology gives us access, in other words, to a vast store of human experience.

New Discoveries and Challenges

Some archaeological stories have only just begun and their tales will unfold and change over the next few decades – from the submerged city of Baiae, one of the most notorious flesh-pots of ancient Rome, to Israel's Tel Zafit National Park, in which lies the ancient city

A detail from one of the mosaic floors discovered in the ruins of the Roman town of Ucetia that was revealed by excavations at Uzès in the south of France.

of Gath, the home town of the biblical Philistine giant, Goliath, to the Mesoamerican city of Tlaxcallan, which Mexico's Centre for Research and Advanced Studies of the National Polytechnic Institute believe was one of several pre-modern societies that were collectively organized and ruled.

In Uzès, in the south of France, an entire new Roman town – Ucetia – has been discovered hidden beneath the car park and surrounding grounds of a provincial school containing artefacts ranging from the 1st century BCE, the era of the Roman Republic, right through to the Middle Ages. While the difficulties in preserving Fort Conger in the Arctic, where Robert Peary was once based and which is now in danger from rising sea levels and salt deterioration, have led the University of Calgary to document the entire site in virtual reality, using three-dimensional imaging techniques.

Excavations can take years; evidence can be misleading. The key to successful archaeology is patience, persistence and an open mind. This book will take you on a journey back in time to visit ancient cultures and view different landscapes. It will also introduce an amazing array of characters, people who have braved desert storms, penetrated terrifying underground tombs and spent entire personal fortunes to bring us face to face with our ancestors. It even takes a detour into bad archaeology, via World War II and the Nazi Party. Archaeology is a vast subject: any period or region could easily fill an entire book, so here we explore this fascinating world through some of archaeology's most exciting highlights.

What is Archaeology?

"Wonderful things," breathed Howard Carter when he first made out the glittering treasures inside Tutankhamun's tomb. The treasure archaeologists find may amaze and delight us, but more important still is the light that scientific study sheds on the past.

The word "archaeology" comes from the Greek words arkhaios (meaning "ancient") and logos (meaning the "word", "reason", or "plan"). The Greeks used the term as early as the 4th century BCE to mean the study of the very ancient past.

Archaeologists often work in multi-disciplinary teams, because it's one of the few areas of enquiry that touches the humanities, natural sciences and social sciences. The study also frequently depends on international partnerships, since today's civilizations don't always respect the boundaries of earlier ones. Archaeologists may also specialize in a certain time period, a geographic area, a

A gold Inca mask. In Inca culture, masks were used either as part of rituals to worship gods such as Inti, the sun god, or as funerary masks.

cultural tradition or some other sub-discipline such as maritime archaeology.

What archaeologists don't do, despite what everyone sees in the media, is study dinosaurs. In the field, it may be difficult to tell the difference between a palaeontologist and an archaeologist – sunhats and shorts look pretty much the same the world over – but archaeologists do not puzzle over titanosaurs or pterodactyls. They would be 65 million years out of their depth. The discovery of dinosaur remains does have a bearing on our understanding of geological, "deep" time, however, and therefore on the history of archaeology.

The material that archaeologists uncover helps them to piece together a living picture of the past. Tools and pottery sherds can tell us huge amounts about the domestic and economic customs of a given civilization; sculptures and artwork enlighten us about religious, spiritual and cultural practices; while weapons and armour offer new insights into ancient warfare.

The difference between history and archaeology comes down to written records. History records the past as set down in writing, oral accounts or documents, while the term "prehistory" covers the period before people began to document their lives. Archaeology spans both. Medieval Europe, with its scribes and scholars, is open to historical study, while the Americas of the same period are the sole concern of archaeology.

Nowadays, archaeologists have a raft of new technologies to aid them in their searches, from aerial photography to ground-penetrating radar, lasers and even robots. These new and ever more sophisticated techniques mean that not only are archaeologists now producing increasingly accurate data, but they are also helping us to rewrite history altogether.

TYPES OF ARCHAEOLOGY

Today, archaeology has obtained a bewildering array of prefixes. There is bioarchaeology, behavioural archaeology, ethnoarchaeology, maritime archaeology and geoarchaeology amongst others. The methods used are as complex and varied as the archaeologists who use them. Nonetheless, whatever their methods, at the heart they aim to illuminate our understanding of the past through studying its material remains. Most prefixes simply refer to the methods used to uncover the past, but here are a few of the most important:

HISTORICAL ARCHAEOLOGY – The study of the material past of civilizations that also created written records.

MARITIME ARCHAEOLOGY – The study of submarine archaeological sites such as shipwrecks and sunken cities.

ETHNOARCHAEOLOGY – The study of modern societies that resemble extinct ones.

AERIAL ARCHAEOLOGY – The study of archaeological sites from aerial photography.

ENVIRONMENTAL ARCHAEOLOGY – The study of relationships between humans and their environment.

PALAEOPATHOLOGY – The study of ancient diseases.

Archaeology Timeline

This timeline aims to give an overview of the periods that this book touches on. It also highlights many, but by no means all, of the most important discoveries and developments in archaeology across the globe. The results of new research and new archaeological finds mean that this is an ever-changing story.

3.3 million years ago
First use of stone tools by early humans

PLIOCENE
2.6 million years ago
c.200,000 years ago
Homo sapiens evolve
c.130,000 years ago
Homo sapiens begin to spread out of Africa
c.40,000 BCE
Neanderthals become extinct
c.20,000 BCE
Pottery emerges in Jiangxi Province, China
c.11,000 BCE
Humans cross the Bering Land Bridge into the Americas

PALAEOLITHIC
10,000 BCE
Temples built in Göbekli Tepe, Turkey
10,000 BCE

MESOLITHIC
5,000 BCE
C.3500 BCE
City states emerge in Sumer
3300 BCE

BRONZE AGE
c.3000 BCE
First writing system, Cuneiform, is developed
c.2800 BCE
Emergence of Indus Valley civilization
c.2560 BCE
The Great Pyramid of Cheops is built in Giza
c.2500 BCE
Stonehenge completed
2000 BCE
1900 BCE
Palace is built at Knossos, Crete
c.1700 BCE
The Shang Dynasty begins in China
1562 BCE
The destruction of Jericho

c.1450 BCE
The Linear B alphabet is used by the Mycenaean culture
c. 1200 BCE
The Fall of Troy
c.780 BCE
Greek colonies established in Asia Minor
753 BCE
Rome is founded

BRONZE AGE
588 BCE
King Nebuchadnezzar of Babylon captures Jerusalem
556 BCE
Babylonian King, Nabonidus, begins excavating temples in Mesopotamia
538 BCE
Persian Empire founded by Cyrus the Great after the conquest of Babylon
c.500 BCE
Candi are created in the Bujung Valley, Malaysia
334 BCE
Alexander the Great invades the Persian empire
221 BCE
Building on the Great Wall of China begins
201 BCE
The Terracotta Army is created following the death of Qin Shi Huang
55 BCE
Caesar invades Britain
0 CE

CLASSICAL CIVILIZATION
9
Battle of Teutoburg Forest
60–1
Boudicca rebels against Roman Rule in Britain
72
Construction of the Colosseum in Rome begins
79
Pompeii is destroyed by the eruption of Mount Vesuvius
122
Construction of Hadrian's wall in Britain begins

220
Three Kingdoms period in China begins
476
The fall of Rome

THE MIGRATION PERIOD (THE DARK AGES)
793
Viking raid on Lindisfarne island
865
Great Heathen Army arrives on English shores
868
The first printed work, the *Diamond Sutra*, is printed in India
899
Tikal is abandoned along with other Mayan cities
1000
c.1000
Leif Erikson reaches L'Anse aux Meadows in Newfoundland

MEDIEVAL ERA
1088
Shen Kuo sets out a theory of archaeology in the Dream Pool Essays
1092
Lü Dalin creates the first archaeological catalogue
c.1150
Angkor Wat is constructed
1368
Ming Dynasty overthrows Mongols
1438
The Inca empire begins after Cuzco's conquest of the Chanka
1440
The rise of the Aztec empire
1485
Battle of Bosworth Field
1521
Tenochtitlan falls to Spanish Conquistadors
1532
Francisco Pizarro conquers the Inca

1607
Jamestown, the first English settlement in the Americas, is founded
1691
The British Levant Company sends an expedition to Palmyra
1700

ENLIGHTENMENT
1707
Edmund Halley attempts to discover the origins of Stonehenge
1721
William Stukeley excavates Stonehenge
1748
Pompeii is excavated by Karl Weber
1799
French soldiers find ancient Egyptian artefacts
1812
Johann Ludwig Burckhardt discovers Petra
1815

INDUSTRIAL ERA
1819
John Smith discovers the Ajanta caves
1822
Champollion deciphers the Rosetta Stone
1826
Charles Masson discovers evidence of the Indus Valley civilization
1834
Stephens and Catherwood uncover the ruins of Mayan cities in the Yucatan jungle
1836
Christian Thomsen explains "The Three Age System" for the first time
1856
Alexander Cunningham founds the Archaeological Survey of India
1861
Johann Fuhlrott discovers the first Neanderthal skeleton

1865
The Palestine Exploration Fund is created
1871
Heinrich Schliemann excavates Troy
1876
The Battle of Little Bighorn
1877
Edward Morse excavates the Omori Shell Mounds
1883
Frederic Ward Putnam begins excavating Serpent Mound in Ohio
1899
Oracle bones are discovered at Yinxu
1900
Divers find the Antikythera mechanism in a shipwreck
1911
Hiram Bingham uncovers Machu Picchu
1914

MODERN ERA
1921
Johan Gunnar Andersson and Yuan Fuli investigate the Yellow River culture in China
1922
Howard Carter discovers Tutankhamun's tomb
1924–26
K. N. Dikshit and John Marshall excavate Mohenjo-Daro
1929
Louis Leakey discovers stone tools in the Olduvai Gorge
1933
Polish archaeologists led by Józef Kostrzewski excavate Biskupin
1938
Heinrich Himmler launches a Nazi archaeological expedition to the Himalayas
1939
Basil Brown excavates the Saxon hoard at Sutton Hoo
1939
Theodore Morde claims to have discovered "The Lost City of the Monkey God"

1940
Marcel Ravidat discovers Lascaux Cave paintings in France
1946
The Dead Sea Scrolls are discovered
1956
Excavation of the Dingling Tomb begins
1962
Excavation of the Manunggul caves in the Philippines begins
1974
Archaeologists in Xi'an, China excavate the Terracotta Army
1978
The Templo Mayor is found beneath the roads of Mexico City
1987
The Nanhai No. 1 ship is found in the South China Sea
1987
Walter Alva saves the Lord of Sipán archaeological site from looters
1994
The Jamestown Rediscovery Project is launched
1996
Kennewick Man is found in the Columbia River in the USA
1998
The "Artognou" stone is unearthed at Tintagel
2008
Marge Konsa excavates Viking ships found at Salme, Estonia
2009
Staffordshire Hoard found from 7th and 8th centuries
2012
The skeleton of King Richard III is found in Leicester
2016
In Sohag, Egypt, a 7,000-year-old city is discovered

PRESENT

A NOTE ABOUT TIME FRAMES

The term BC refers to "Before Christ", meaning before the
year Jesus Christ was born, while AD refers to "Anno Domini",
meaning "the year of our Lord". The religious connotations
of these terms can cause concern, particularly when discussing
cultures outside Europe. The terms BCE and CE are meant
to sidestep the problem. They simply mean "Before the
Common Era" and "Common Era". As the most commonly
used calendar is the Christian one, they are in effect identical
to the previous system.

A Fascination with the Past

The very first people to discover the great tombs of Egypt were driven not by curiosity but by greed. They were literally gold diggers, opportunistic thieves. Although the Pharaohs and the zealous priests who guarded the tombs did everything they could to warn the robbers off, they met with little success. An inscription in the tomb of Vizier Khentika Ikhekhi at Saqqara – behind two sets of false doors – reads:

"As for all men who shall enter this my tomb… there will be judgment… an end shall be made for him."

A papyrus documenting a trial, and the "double-rod" beating before it, from the time of Ramesses IX (1142–23 BCE) tells us that thieves broke into hundreds of tombs, including those of Amenophis III, Seti I and Ramesses II. The confessions of the stonecutter Hap, the water carrier Kemwese, the artisan Iramen, the peasant Amenemheb and the Negro slave Thenefer give a graphic account of the problem the pharaohs faced: "We opened their coffins and their coverings. We found the august mummy of this king… there was a numerous string of amulets and ornaments of gold at its throat; its head had a mask of gold upon it… We stripped off the gold, we found the king's wife likewise and stripped off all that we found. We… stole their furniture, being vases of gold, silver and bronze."

Even today, villagers from modern-day Gurnah, which is built over and around the remarkable ruins at Karnak in Upper Egypt, have been imprisoned for scavenging the treasure that Egypt now regards as its national heritage.

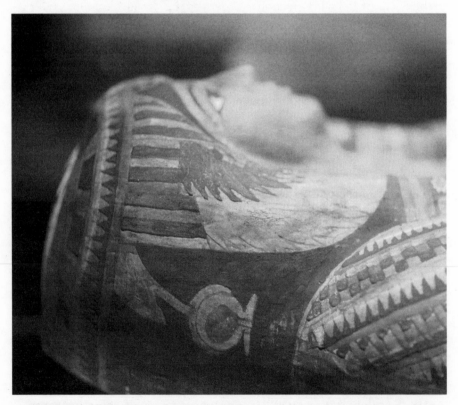

This colourful Egyptian mummy survives intact, but many were desecrated and the sanctity of their tombs destroyed by thieves. Lured by wealth beyond their dreams, the robbers broke through every barrier and took precious metals to be melted down.

There has always been tension between the desire to collect the treasures of ancient cultures and the yearning to understand what they say about human life. The two instincts might seem contradictory, but perhaps one reason why archaeology is so popular is that it serves both of these perfectly human impulses well.

Many of the prized historic objects we now put on pedestals in museums were once pure loot. The Roman Emperor Constantine helped himself to the very tallest obelisk from the magnificent temple complex at Karnak and installed it in the middle of Rome (where it is now known as the Lateran Obelisk). Alexander the Great plundered the jewel of Persia, Persepolis, known as the "wealthiest city under the sun". Even the sublime alert bronze horses that crown Venice's Basilica of Saint Mark were stolen from Constantinople during the Crusades. Somehow, they never made it back. Looted in turn by Napoléon, they were removed to Paris, and then returned – to Venice – on his downfall.

In 16th-century England, Dr Dee, Elizabeth I's handsome alchemist-cum-astrologer and advisor, straddled both camps. Dee claimed to predict the future, talking to angels through the swirling reflections he called up from a sinister "magic" mirror. We now know this was a piece of polished obsidian, once used in the ancient rituals of an Aztec god. How Dr Dee came by such a precious thing we do not know; the Spanish conquistadors probably stole it in South America.

During the Renaissance, rich Italian families began amassing large collections of ancient classical art, much of which was lying buried beneath their feet. Lorenzo de' Medici's famous library and gardens in Florence were full of ancient Greek and Roman sculpture. In Aix-en-Provence, the great intellectual Nicolas-Claude Fabri de Peiresc turned his entire home into a gallery and museum of

Classical works. As European royal families struggled to establish national and military supremacy, ancient art became a quick way of both making money and also acquiring a veneer of legitimacy. In the 15th century, King Matthias I of Hungary kept his huge collection of Roman antiquities at Szombathely, a castle built with stone from the town's Roman baths. It is still there, and now a museum.

Eventually, there came a dawning interest in actually studying history and culture to understand them, and a realization that the great monuments of civilization should not be lost. In the early 16th century Pope Leo X commissioned the painter Raphael to study and document all the monuments of Rome, putting an end to the uncontrolled plunder of the city's rich heritage.

The "Cabinet of Curiosities"

In 1605, a young Danish physician and natural philosopher, Ole Worm, inherited a fortune and set out across Europe to continue his education. Worm became one of the world's first serious scientific collectors, creating what could be called the first museum.

A philosopher, physician and dedicated linguist, Worm's defining characteristic was his amazing, boundless curiosity – and his painstakingly accurate methodology. By studying with a new scientific rigour subjects such as "unicorns' horns" or the evolutionary adaptation of birds of paradise, Worm pre-empted the rational values of the coming Age of Enlightenment by a hundred years.

Nationalism also played its part. A wide-ranging report that Worm wrote on the ancient monuments of Denmark aroused the interest of King Frederik III. Frederik realized that this cultural heritage could be useful in uniting the uneasy "Two Kingdoms" of Norway and Denmark. The use of science, culture and archaeology

A "cabinet of curiosities" from a private collection. It includes some coral, a Buddhist idol and skulls of a macaw, an ostrich and a human medical specimen. If this were not eclectic enough, there are also a Chinese clock, giant barnacles and a mammoth tooth.

as potent propaganda tools in Scandinavia set a precedent in Europe, although this did not prevent Frederik from commissioning a throne chair made entirely from the horns of the mythical "unicorn" 30 years after Worm had correctly identified them as narwhal horns.

Ranging from fossils to stuffed animals, along with bizarre ethnographic treasures found in the New World, this hugely influential Renaissance man's collection, and the documentation that went with it, helped bridge the divide between science and mere curiosity. Which does not mean there were not some very curious exhibits: Worm owned what may well have been the world's first robot, a *statua librata pondre mobilis* – a wheeled figure with flexible limbs that could pick things up – as well as an "egg" supposedly laid by a Norwegian, Anna Omundsdatter. The egg came with sworn witness testimonials as to its miraculous appearance, including one by a parish priest.

As a naturalist and antiquarian, Worm was in the vanguard of a developing wave of scientific enquiry across Europe. The significance of this for archaeology lay in the way that he categorized and ordered his vast collection. Apart from coins and objects that were unclassifiable, he listed the eclectic mix of things by their different materials: clay, wood, bronze, stone, iron and so on. This set a precedent for more rigorous enquiry.

In response to the methodology by which Worm ordered his collections, another Dane, Christian Jürgensen Thomsen, developed the Three Ages dating system (still used today) as a way of classifying archaeological finds. As director of the Royal Museum of Nordic Antiquities in Copenhagen, Thomsen was keen to display objects from prehistory in a rational order that would help people understand them. He came up with the relative system of a Stone Age, Bronze Age and Iron Age, based on the main technologies that people were using at different times. Even if dating systems are now far more complex, this was a real innovation.

Worm's extraordinary collection was later part of the Royal Danish Kunstkammer (Art Chamber). His "cabinet" has been painstakingly recreated by the artist Rosamond Purcell at the Natural History Museum of Denmark in Copenhagen, where polar bears and crocodiles hang from rafters, and skulls (both animal and human) vie for shelf space with exotic shells and beads.

Soon, the aristocracy of Europe followed Worm's lead. Every educated gentleman had his own "cabinet of curiosities" or Wunderkammern, part witch's cave, part scientific laboratory and apothecary's chamber. Even the great artist Rembrandt turned much of his studio into a trove of curiosities.

Between 1688 and 1815, the European naval powers of Spain, the Netherlands, Great Britain and France competed for power and influence, fighting five wars in the process. The empire-builders became just as obsessed with collecting things as they were with dominating new lands. The world's first museums, which would become driving forces in the development of archaeology, were built on the back of "curious" collections like these.

CHRISTIAN JÜRGENSEN THOMSEN (1788–1865)

In 1816 Thomsen, a Danish antiquarian – primarily a collector of coins – of independent means was selected to curate the first exhibition for the Danish Royal Commission for the Collection and Preservation of Antiquities. He made the decision to organize the items in the exhibition according to their age where previously they might have been sorted according to their materials or the sophistication of their craftsmanship. Thomsen decided that his task was to determine in which periods the artefacts had been made.

By mapping out which kinds of phenomena occurred at the same time in deposits and which did not, he was able to define trends that were typical of certain periods. He found that stone tools occurred with amber, pottery and glass beads, whereas bronze was found with both iron and gold, but silver was only found with iron. He also discovered that bronze weapons did not occur with iron artefacts so each

period could be defined by the material from which tools
or utensils were made. How and where items were found
were the key to dating them as was keeping items together,
allowing Thomsen to build a chronological framework for
the materials in the collection and to classify new finds in
relation to the established chronology, even without much
knowledge of its provenance. His chronology was established
by 1825, and visitors to the museum were instructed in
his methods. Thomsen also published journal articles and
pamphlets in which he emphasized the importance of the find
circumstances for later interpretation and dating. Finally, in
1836, he published his Guide to Northern Antiquity, which
formalized his chronology together with comments about
which items occurred together in finds.

A Royal First

The man who must surely count as the world's first archaeologist
was the enigmatic Nabû-nā'id; also known as Nabonidus, he reigned
over Babylon, the most famous city in ancient Mesopotamia, during
556–539 BCE.

Nabonidus ruled a vast empire that stretched from the Persian
Gulf to the borders of modern-day Egypt. If he had wanted to
succeed as king, he should have spent his time organizing armies,
pleasing his people and quashing opposition. Instead, he set off into
the desert to uncover and restore archaeological wonders, leaving
his feckless son Belshazzar in charge. A remarkable find from the
ruins of an ancient temple confirms not just the story of Nabonidus,
but also the fate of Belshazzar.

Until the discovery of the Nabonidus Cylinder, no mention of

Belshazzar had been found outside of the Book of Daniel in the Bible; as far as official history was concerned, no such person had ever really existed. In 1881, the Assyriologist Hormuzd Rassam discovered a piece of baked clay (a cylinder, now in the Pergamon Museum in Berlin, with a copy in the British Museum) that proved otherwise, in a desert temple. Nabonidus, it transpired, had buried an eloquent record of his existence.

Rassam found the cylinder in ancient Sippar, a cult religious centre whose temple was already more than 2,000 years old when Nabonidus took the throne. Before burying his cylinder, Nabonidus inscribed it with a heartfelt prayer: "As for Belshazzar the eldest son – my offspring – instil reverence for your great godhead in his heart. May he not commit a cultic mistake. May he be sated with a life of plenitude."

Nabonidus describes how, "with the craft of the exorcist", he rediscovered the ancient moon-god temples, and set about restoring them. He repaired at least three temples and a pyramid, as well as preserving King Aššurbanipal's treasure.

Belshazzar allowed Babylon to fall into the hands of the Persians: on 29 October 539 BCE, the city fell to Cyrus the Great, the legendary Persian leader. Belshazzar was almost certainly executed, and Nabonidus was exiled, characterized by the Persians as a lying, uncultured fool.

His fate prefigures a key problem in archaeology: how can one protect places of great antiquity from the forces of destruction? Time has not been kind to Babylon or to ancient Mesopotamia. In recent times, while killing and displacing hundreds of thousands of people, so-called "Islamic State" (or Daesh) extremists have looted and destroyed many archaeological sites and there has been a systematic cultural and religious cleansing campaign across northern Iraq and Syria.

Lessons from the Past

Across the world, interest in the past has waxed and waned. The educated classes of Song Dynasty China (960–1279 CE) believed that the discovery of ancient artefacts could be used in state events. This attitude was criticized, but at the same time it was acknowledged that the objects proved useful by providing information on ancient techniques.

In Renaissance Europe from the 14th century onwards, there was renewed interest in classical culture. Scholars and historians – such as Flavio Biondo (who studied under Ballistario of Cremona and published a series of encyclopaedias) and the artist and architect Leon Battista Alberti – set about documenting the ruins of ancient Rome. In England, the antiquarian and historian William Camden began making a list of monuments as part of a topographical survey he started in 1577. Meanwhile in the Americas, the Spanish had begun to establish rule over vast swathes of land and were discovering the treasures of the indigenous peoples, such as the Maya.

An Appetite for Adventure

The modern world's first major archaeological expedition began as one big adventure. On the morning of 4 October 1691, a group of 30 men arrived at the ancient city of Palmyra, in the middle of the Syrian desert. Through a fringe of palm trees, an exotic vision of graceful arches, courts and ruined temples rose out of the creamy sands: the home of the legendary King Solomon. At its heart was a great colonnade, a street lined with gracious Corinthian columns.

They had reached one of the most important cultural centres of the ancient world in the 1st–2nd century CE, an opulent caravan oasis. With its place on the Silk Road and intermittently under the rule of classical Rome, Palmyra had been a cultural powerhouse. Its

The Temple of Ba'al in Palmyra, particularly admired by William Halifax during the 1691 expedition. It is feared to have been flattened in 2015 by Islamic extremists, who beheaded its retired chief of antiquities.

buildings are strongly original in style, uniting Graeco-Roman art with Persian and even Asian influences.

William Halifax, a one-time chaplain of the Syrian city of Aleppo, admired the extraordinary great Temple of Ba'al. He found a few hundred "miserable people" living among the ruins in dirt shacks, along with their sheikh. "I question somewhat whether any City in the World could have challenged Precedence over this in its Glory," he noted.

The group's report was the first documented account of Palmyra, published by the Royal Society in London four years later. It reached a large audience not just in Britain but also in France, the Netherlands and Italy. In it was the first image of Palmyra to reach European eyes: a 180-degree view of the entire city.

The intellectual élite of the West was set afire by the oasis city's stark beauty, kick-starting a frenetic new fashion for neoclassicism. James Dawkins and Robert Wood travelled there in 1751, gentlemen scholars from the Society of Dilettantes. Their romantic depictions of heroic adventures in the desert inspired the "cult of the sublime" – a Europe-wide love affair with ruins.

This was the first Western contact with Palmyra for hundreds of years, and whetted appetites for more romantic "discoveries"; a story that would end up inspiring travellers like the Swiss explorer Johann Ludwig Burckhardt, who discovered the glorious, isolated ruins of Petra in the Jordanian desert.

Sadly, Palmyra has suffered greatly since Halifax first saw it in the 17th century. Its Arch of Triumph was deliberately destroyed by so-called Islamic State in 2015. Although 3D technology has allowed it to be re-sculpted from Egyptian marble, using photographs and drawings as a source, this kind of reconstruction is controversial, but shows just how much modern technology can achieve.

An Appetite for Antiquaries: Making History

It was 1707: the first meeting of the British Society of Antiquaries, at the Bear Tavern on the Strand, in the heart of London. It was the world's first such society, and William Stukeley served as its first secretary.

Fascinated by Stonehenge's solar alignment, he and the renowned astronomer Edmund Halley attempted to date the stones and studied the monument in depth, on site. Their calculations were wrong, but their investigations were nevertheless a key moment in field archaeology. Stukeley's skilled drawings are still used in studies of Stonehenge today.

The society that Stukeley helped create tried to get Britain to follow the lead of Sweden, where archaeological sites were already protected by royal statute. It helped establish archaeology's roots in science and observation, and eventually drew up the first UK legislation protecting ancient monuments.

The society also campaigned against the increasing dilapidation of Stonehenge. After Stukeley's time, new housing started to encroach on the monument. An entire trilithon toppled in 1797, and one of the upright sarsens of the outer circle later fell down, along with its lintel. Would this remarkable monument, an icon the world over, survive?

Overseas, meanwhile, other such societies followed the British Antiquaries' example. In India, William Jones founded the Asiatic Society in 1784 and began research into the country's history and other parts of the "Orient". The society eventually handed over its collections to the Indian Museum, which was established in 1814.

WILLIAM STUKELEY
(1687–1765)

A doctor by training, and later an ordained clergyman, William Stukeley's ideas on archaeology and his detailed recording of sites of archaeological importance, in particular of the stone circles at Avebury and Stonehenge, were influential in the development of its study in the later 18th and early 19th centuries. He formed a passion for old ruins and monuments while a medical student and every year from 1710 to 1725 he went on an archaeological tour of Britain, seeking out various features and buildings of interest. In about 1722 Stukeley became fascinated with the stone circles at Stonehenge and

Avebury in Wiltshire, possibly as a result of reading John Aubrey's *Monumenta Britannica* which mentioned Avebury. Throughout the early 1720s, Stukeley visited Avebury making records that proved of great importance to later archaeologists as a number of the features he noted were lost over time – for example, the destruction of some of the megaliths by local people for building material.

It was while at Avebury in 1723 that Stukeley began a draft of the *History of the Temples of the Ancient Celts*, drawing on his fieldwork at Avebury and Stonehenge as well as his field-notes from other prehistoric sites. In 1724, he returned to Avebury and Stonehenge but 1725 was the last year that he did any fieldwork there. From the 1720s, it seems that he believed that Avebury was laid out to represent a snake with its head and tail. By 1724, he argued that the snake was a symbol of Christ, with its shedding of skin echoing the resurrection and the circle or head representing the unity and wholeness of God. Using his friend Edmund Halley's arguments about the gradual shift in the compass over time, Stukeley calculated that Stonehenge was built in 460 BCE and Avebury in 1860 BCE.

In 1740, he published *Stonehenge*, a book that he described as being devoted to the subject of "Patriarchal

Christianity". He believed that learned people would read the book to educate themselves about stone circles and druids, and that in doing so they would encounter the ancient proto-Christianity of Britain and thus recognize how similar it was to modern Anglicanism. At the same time, he was starting to depict the stone circles at Avebury, which are actually circular, as ovals in his illustrations so that they better fitted the shape of a serpent's head, which he believed they symbolized.

While his beliefs on the building of the henges by druids, and his ideas on the form of their religion were largely discredited towards the end of his life and later, Stukeley remains important for having started a discourse on the subject, and for creating interest in the study of prehistoric monuments and other items of archaeological interest.

A New Dawn?

In the early 1770s, Thomas Jefferson, the principal author of the US Declaration of Independence, began what was probably the very first modern-style archaeological excavation, to test the accuracy of a theory.

Jefferson decided to examine a mysterious earthwork near his home Monticello, one of a cluster of 13 huge mounds in Virginia's Shenandoah Valley. It was known locally as Monasukapanough. John Smith, the English leader of the Jamestown Virginia colony, had named the area Monacan Indian territory. The indigenous peoples called it Amai Amañuhkañ, the "Country of the People of the Land". By this time, however, Virginia's native tribes had all but melted into the landscape. The settlers found the landscape dotted with enigmatic mounds, some huge, often built in symbolic animal or snake-like shapes that Native Americans were not considered "civilized" enough to have built.

It was argued the builders must have been a "lost race" – variously claimed to be the Vikings, Phoenicians, Tartars, Chinese, Welsh or even the "lost tribes of Israel". Jefferson believed otherwise. When he was eight years old, he had seen a group of Indians approach the mound with what he took to be sorrow. They knew precisely the location of the monument, and how to find their way through the woods. Linking the tribesmen in this way was a significant insight, because it contradicted the "lost race" theory.

The 16th-century Spanish explorer Hernando de Soto had wondered if the flat-topped mounds could be the bases of temples. Remembering what he had seen, Jefferson, a formidable personality with opinions to match, was sure they were Native American monuments that had been built for ceremonial purposes.

Jefferson was the first to specify and then test an archaeological hypothesis, seeking answers to specific questions. Crucially, he wanted to know if the "Indian Grave" was a ceremonial burial site, where Indians re-buried their dead standing up, as he believed. He also wondered if the burials could have taken place over hundreds of years. He used two excavation strategies: trenching, which let him see the mound's internal structure, and stratigraphy, a method that put the American founding father about 100 years ahead of his time.

"I first dug superficially in several parts of it, and came to collections of human bones... These were lying in the utmost confusion, some vertical, some oblique, some horizontal, and directed to every point of the compass," he wrote in a painstaking record of his results. We now know that the mounds mostly date back to the late prehistoric and "early contact" era (c.900–1700 CE).

Meanwhile, the Indian story moved west, following the ever-expanding frontier. In 1935, gold diggers became grave robbers when a group of miners blew up the largest of eastern Oklahoma's Spiro Mounds with gunpowder. They found – and sold – so many artefacts that the site became known as the "King Tut of the West".

An Emperor in Egypt

Why do there seem to be at least as many mummies in France as there are in Egypt? Sitting in the Louvre Museum in Paris is an entire "Temple Room", as well as a "Sarcophagus Room". The museum holds works of Egyptian art including the wonderful Crypt of the Sphinx, the Zodiac of Dendera and the famous Tod treasure, unearthed from a village near Luxor. Meanwhile, in London, the British Museum holds the Rosetta Stone and the incredible monumental sculpture of Ramesses II. Between them, the two institutions possess thousands of magnificent, truly priceless works of Egyptian art as well as smaller items. The collections in London and Paris are a legacy of the long and bitter power struggle between the British and the French. In the 19th century, the two dominant imperial powers fought over the world's cultural capital, filling up their museums as they went. Statue by statue, tomb by tomb, the rivals engaged in a huge game of archaeological one-upmanship. It was a novel way to wage war. Other countries, such as Germany and Austria, weren't far behind, while the Italian Charles Emmanuel III of Turin had already looted 300 items from the Karnak area.

Having led the French into Italy with ease and made Venice "Europe's drawing room", Napoléon Bonaparte was the talk of Europe. He decided to strike England a fatal blow by stabbing at the soft underbelly of the British empire, seizing control of the land trade route to India. Egypt would be the blade.

On 19 May 1798, Bonaparte sailed from Italy with an army

of nearly 54,000 men. With them was another, smaller army of scientists, engineers, artists and linguists – their task to capture not Egyptian soil but Egyptian culture. Napoléon called them his Savants, or "Wise Men". It was the world's first large-scale scientific expedition.

The French landed on 2 July and came upon Cairo, a vision from *A Thousand and One Nights*. Between them and their glittering goal was an army of Mameluke soldiers, mounted on noble Arab horses and armed with silver-hilted, curved yataghan sabres. The Ottomans had ruled in Egypt for more than 500 years, supported by this ferocious warrior élite class. Before the ensuing battle, Napoléon famously gestured at the stern geometry of the pyramids and the Horizon of Khufu looming 467 ft (142 m) behind them. "Soldiers," he said, "forty centuries are looking down on you!" The French won the day.

When the emperor's army came upon the ancient city of Thebes, with its remarkable temples, an emotion électrique ran through the soldiers, who burst into spontaneous applause. By August they had taken most of Upper Egypt. Ultimately, though, it was the Savants who claimed the greater victory. While the men suffered, the Savants explored. They mapped, drew, measured and surveyed.

Artist Dominique-Vivant Denon was the first to draw the temples and ruins at Thebes, Esna, Edfu and Philae. His book of meticulously drawn engravings, which went into 40 editions, set off a wave of Egypt-mania in Europe. Ancient Greece and Rome had always been seen as the definitive prototypes of Western civilization. Now there was an alternative. This was the beginning of an entire branch of archaeology, with its own special name, Egyptology.

As Napoléon's army plundered Egypt, a man named Thomas Bruce, Lord Elgin, hadn't forgotten Greece and Greek art.

Britain's ambassador to Constantinople, Elgin bought a permit and removed what was left of the marble frieze on the Parthenon in Athens. Sections of it had been ground up and used as mortar by the occupying Ottoman Turks. In 1812, Elgin transported the sculptures to Britain, skirting bankruptcy in the process; his actions ensured that the Elgin Marbles suffered no further damage in the Greek War of Independence.

Fetish for Pharaohs

In the Anglo–French rivalry for empire, India and Egypt were the key prizes. In 1816, Henry Salt arrived in Egypt as British Consul General. For Salt, this was an opportunity to make money: lots of it. Bernardino Drovetti, an Italian who had served under Napoléon, was his opposite number in the French camp. With untold riches at stake, archaeology was about to become a whole new battlefield.

Egypt was thick with adventurers, rogues and mavericks who could scent a fortune in the sands. Enthusiastic and scholarly collectors like the wealthy dilettante Sir William Bankes, intent on bagging an obelisk for his English country garden, were also on the prowl. The cast of characters included the Swiss explorer Johann Ludwig Burckhardt, fresh from two years travelling in disguise as "The Sheikh" Ibrahim ibn Abdallah. Burckhardt had made expeditions to Palmyra, Damascus and Baalbek and into the untamed lands of Hauran in Syria/Jordan. He had also made two sensational discoveries: the first was the abandoned Nabataean city of Petra in Jordan, and the second was the great sand-swept temple at Abu Simbel, in Nubia in southern Egypt. Burckhardt fell in with a strange Italian from Padua, a water engineer who was on his uppers. It was Burckhardt who would introduce the "Great Belzoni" to Salt. Thus began the "War of the Consuls".

Egypt's ruthless ruler Pasha Muhammad Ali was struggling to establish the country as a modern nation. He was quite happy to exchange the past for the present. Ali cunningly played the consuls of the world's two most dangerous and predatory nations off against each other for Egyptian gain.

Born in Padua, the son of a barber, Belzoni had a hugely colourful and varied career. He first apparently studied hydraulics, while contemplating taking monastic vows, before working as a barber in the Netherlands. A giant of a man at 6 ft 7 in (2 m) tall, in 1803 Belzoni fled to England, married a woman called Sarah Bane and

Giovanni Belzoni in Arab dress.

along with his new wife, joined a travelling circus. They performed demonstrations of strength and agility at fairs and on the streets of London and later appeared at Astley's amphitheatre where he used magic lanterns in his shows.

Belzoni was the most unlikely Egyptologist in the world, but Burckhardt saw beneath the surface: this was a very determined man with a range of rare skills, particularly when it came to engineering. Belzoni delighted in the explorer's stories, one of which concerned the head of the "Young Memnon", which lay separated from its colossal body in the burning sands on the west bank of the Nile. It was an effigy of "Ozymandias", the Greek name for Ramesses II, and the inspiration behind Shelley's sonnet.

Armed with Burckhardt's information, Belzoni rampaged around Egypt, trying to stay one step ahead of Drovetti and his sidekick, the military deserter Jean-Jacques Rifaud. The French had been granted a licence to excavate at Thebes, and the remarkable complex at Karnak that the Egyptians knew as Ipet Issu ("the most select of places") – a fact that infuriated Salt, who knew that they had stolen a march on him.

Burckhardt and Belzoni persuaded Salt that the "Young Memnon", stuck in the desert near Thebes, should be resurrected and given to the British Museum. Napoleon's army had already tried to move the statue, using gunpowder "to blow off its wig", and found it an impossible task.

Unfortunately for Belzoni, Drovetti was one step ahead of him. When he asked the local bey (provincial general) for permission to remove the statue, Drovetti arrived in person. He told Belzoni that no labour would be made available to help in the enormous task. Undeterred and ever-resourceful, Belzoni realized that the best way to move the statue was to use the Nile's waters. He also realized that

No easy task: the "Great Belzoni" and his workmen haul away at the "Young Memnon".

there was a ticking clock: the great river would flood in a month's time. The race was on. Belzoni found the statue and proceeded to hire 80 labourers of his own. With 14 wooden poles, four palm-leaf ropes and four sledge rollers, he set about moving Ozymandias.

He often worked at night avoiding the daytime heat: he levered rollers underneath the statue front and back. Some dragged, some pulled; no doubt Belzoni added his great strength. Then everyone hauled the pink granite statue inch by inch towards the river, moving the back roller to the front as they progressed.

After a month of waiting for Salt's promised boat to turn up, Rifaud arrived aboard a large boat bound for Aswan. He refused Belzoni use of the boat. Every day, the Nile was getting lower, and even Belzoni's bribes had ceased to have any effect on the locals:

he could not get out of Thebes. Until Drovetti made the mistake of presenting another local dignitary, the Casheff of Erments, with a jar of sardines. The casheff was outraged by such a pathetic gift. Heaping Belzoni with lavish praise, he invited the strongman and his English wife, Sarah, to a feast. The Great Belzoni would get all the help he wanted, could take any boat he wanted – any statues, for that matter. Never one to turn down an opportunity, Belzoni grabbed a few statues from Karnak for good measure, built a mud ramp down to the Nile – where for one heart-stopping moment the "Young Memnon" sank into the mud – and set off with Sarah for Cairo.

Belzoni had caught the bug. Using methods that would make a modern archaeologist scream – he thought nothing of opening sealed tombs with a battering ram – he plundered everything of value in sight. He dug through 20 ft (6 m) of hardened sand to get at the monuments of Abu Simbel, rediscovered the entrance to the Great Pyramid and found five tombs in the Valley of the Kings, including that of Seti I, thereby paving the way for a long series of important excavations that others could now undertake.

Belzoni's later archaeological exploits were prodigious. He made further investigations into the great temple of Edfu, visited Elephantine and Philae, cleared sand from the great temple at Abu Simbel, undertook excavations at Karnak, and opened up the tomb of Seti I. He was the first to go into the depths of the second pyramid of Giza. In 1820 he published an account of his work in England, the *Narrative of the Operations and Recent Discoveries within the Pyramids, Temples, Tombs and Excavations in Egypt and Nubia, &c* the following year. In 1820–22 he showed facsimiles of the sepulchre of Seti I in London and Paris.

The following year he made for West Africa, proposing to travel to Timbuktu. Refused permission to pass through Morocco, he went instead via the Guinea Coast and although he reached Benin, he died of dysentery just a short while later. The traveller Richard Burton contended that Belzoni had in fact been robbed and murdered. In 1829 his widow published his drawings of the royal tombs at Thebes.

In 1844, the American vice-consul, George Gliddon, made an emotional appeal. All this pillaging had to stop: "Words cannot express our rage… about all the demolition that has taken place here [at Karnak]."

Fortunately, there were signs of a new, more thoughtful approach developing among individuals who would approach Egypt's majestic past with greater respect. The new cast included a French artist named Frédéric Cailliaud, who would diligently copy hundreds of ancient documents and papyri. William Bankes also copied thousands of inscriptions, in situ, including the name of Ramesses II. The efforts of these two men, one French and one English, eventually helped a young man called Champollion to decipher the Rosetta Stone.

JOHANN LUDWIG BURCKHARDT (1784–1817)

Burckhardt was born in Lausanne, Switzerland to a family of wealthy Basel silk merchants. He studied at Leipzig and Göttingen, travelling to England in 1806 in search of employment with the civil service. Instead, he joined an expedition with the African Association to resolve problems with the course of the Niger River. To prepare he studied Arabic, science and medicine at Cambridge University and began to adopt Arabic dress. In 1809 he went to Syria to finesse his knowledge of Arabic and Muslim customs. On the way he learned of a man called Ulrich Jasper Seetzen, who had gone in search of the lost city of Petra, but had been poisoned. In Syria he called himself Sheikh Ibrahim Ibn Abdallah to mask his identity and investigated languages and archaeological sites. He became the first European to discover Hittite or Luwian hieroglyphs. After two years living as a Muslim, Burckhardt felt he could travel safely. Journeys to Syria, Lebanon, Palestine and Transjordan confirmed the success of his disguise. Leaving Aleppo in early 1812 he headed south through Damascus, Ajloun and Amman.

On the road to Cairo he heard rumours of ancient ruins in a narrow valley close to the supposed biblical tomb of Aaron, brother to Moses. Telling his guide that he wanted to sacrifice a goat to Aaron, Burckhardt was led through the narrow valley. On 22 August 1812, he became the first modern European to see the extraordinary ancient Nabataean city of Petra. He wrote, "It appears very probable that the ruins in Wady Mousa are those of the ancient Petra ... Of this at least I am persuaded, from all the information I procured, that there is no other ruin between the extremities of the Dead sea and Red sea, of sufficient importance to answer to that city. Whether or not I have discovered the remains of the capital of Arabia Petraea, I leave to the decision of Greek scholars." He was unable to stay long at the ruins or take significant notes as he feared that his true identity would be revealed.

Continuing his travels, Burckhardt arrived in Cairo on 4 September 1812. After four months in Cairo, he decided to journey up the Nile to Upper Egypt and Nubia. He persuaded his employer that the information he would collect on African cultures would help in his planned journey to West Africa. In January 1813 he departed Cairo to travel towards Dongola in

The remarkable hidden enclave of Petra in the Jordanian desert. Burckhardt's were the first Western eyes to see it.

modern-day Sudan. He was stopped by hostile peoples less than 160 km (100 miles) from his goal. Travelling north, he found the ruins of the Great Temple of Ramesses II at Abu Simbel in March 1813. As the temple was choked with sand, he was unable to excavate the entrance. His friend Giovanni Belzoni returned in 1817 to complete excavations. Burckhardt made an additional trip to Nubia as far as Shendi near the Pyramids of Meroë, from where he travelled to the Red Sea.

Entering Jeddah in June 1814, Burckhardt became sick with dysentery but, having proved his credentials as a Muslim, he was allowed to travel to Mecca. He spent several months there performing rituals associated with the Hajj, writing detailed notes about the city and the culture of the local people. On a later trip to Medina he become sick with dysentery again and leaving Arabia, he arrived exhausted on the Sinai peninsula before returning to Cairo.

In the last two years of his life Burckhardt edited his journals, and prepared for a caravan that would take him west across the Sahara to Timbuktu and the Niger river. He travelled to Alexandria and to Mount Sinai where he visited St Catherine's Monastery before returning to Cairo. Overcome again with dysentery he died in Cairo on 15 October 1817, never having reached the Niger. Buried as a Muslim, the stone that marks his grave bears his Muslim name.

Burckhardt sent his journals of his travels back to England on a regular basis along with a significant collection of letters, so much detail on his journeys has been preserved. By the time of his death at the age of 33 he had amassed a collection of 800 oriental manuscripts which were later bequeathed to Cambridge University.

Greece and the Democratic Ideal

Together, the pen and the sword galvanized the first ever formal excavations in Greece.

When Johann Joachim Winckelmann wrote his influential *History of the Art of Antiquity* he portrayed classical – mainly Greek – art as the pinnacle of European civilization. The German cobbler's son was riding a wave of intellectual curiosity fed by Greece's isolation under Ottoman rule.

To European societies, the classical civilizations of Greece and Rome embodied the best of civic and artistic virtues. Indeed, the excavations of Pompeii, which had begun in the mid-1700s, had become a significant tourist destination. Democratic ideals were the silent symbolism behind many of the new public buildings in France, Britain and the fledgling USA. Winckelmann added to that the notion that a society's civil success was pinned to the quality, or "nobility", of its art. The evolution of art, he argued, paralleled the life cycle of civilizations.

Pro-Greek sentiment was exploding across Europe, fuelled by accounts of atrocities committed by the occupying Ottomans. The British colonel Martin William Leake was sent on a spying mission: he brought back booty which is now mainly in the Fitzwilliam Museum, in Cambridge.

In 1811, as Elgin was busily transporting the Acropolis's marbles across the Mediterranean, a group of amateur archaeologists forged a multicultural friendship that would finally put the archaeology first. The German architects Jacob Linkh, Otto Magnus von Stackelberg and Carl von Hallerstein met English counterparts John Foster and Charles Robert Cockerell in Athens. Rome had long been part of the Grand Tour, a kind of open-air finishing school for rich young gentlemen, but now Athens, too, was de rigueur. The group made drawings at the Acropolis, in Sounion and on the island of Aegina, where Hallerstein excavated at the Temple and the Jupiter Panhellenion. Although Hallerstein removed some of the remains to the Glyptothek in Munich, the group had done valuable work in documenting and publicizing important ancient Greek sites. They consolidated the work of the 18th-century architectural historians Stuart and Revett, and cemented the long archaeological love affair between the Prussians, the English and Greece.

With admirable clarity of ambition, the German government

Athens's magnificent Parthenon temple, standing on the rocky outcrop of the Acropolis. To visitors in the eighteenth and nineteenth centuries this building seemed to epitomize spirituality and unity, but in fact it was once a riot of colour, not the pared-down structure seen today. Teams of international excavators have competed to work here.

funded a scientific expedition to Olympia directed by a young historian, Ernst Curtius. In a world first, it was agreed that artefacts were to remain in Greece, according to contracts drawn up between the Greek and German governments. Curtius was given the support of the best German archaeologists of the period, including Friedrich Adler and Wilhelm Dorpfeld.

Six years later, most of the buildings reported by Pausanias had been cleared and identified, including the Heraion, the Temple of Zeus, the Metroon, the Philippeion, the precinct of Pelops and the Echo Colonnade. With its own national identity, Greece could now enact its own laws. It would no longer be possible to simply come and remove the great treasures of Hellenic culture without so much as a protest. There would still be some figures, though, who would try to do so, including one spectacularly unscrupulous adventurer: Heinrich Schliemann.

The Siege of Troy

Heinrich Schliemann had decided to devote his life to a great mystery: the *Iliad*, Homer's epic poem about the kidnapping of the beautiful Helen and the ten-year siege of Troy. Was Troy a real city, and if so, could it be found?

In 1858, at the age of 36 and wealthy due to trading in gold dust, Schliemann was rich beyond dreams. He met Frank Calvert, a quiet and unassuming diplomat who was an expert on Homer. For 20 years, Calvert had studied the "Troad", near the Dardenelles, drawing sites, comparing records and trying to convince the British Museum to fund excavations. He believed that he had found the legendary site of Troy within a prominent "tell", or mound, at Hissarlik. The Persian ruler Xerxes, Alexander the Great Ottoman and Sultan Mehmed II had all recognized this as the site of Troy.

Calvert's trial trenches suggested that the site had twice been burned to the ground, fitting with Homer's account.

Scenting an opportunity for fame, Schliemann became officially enamoured with the legend of Troy, claiming it had been a boyhood obsession. He became the Englishman's business partner – and then took over.

Schliemann's first finds were modest, made under the watchful eye of a Turkish official, Amin Effendi: clay cups and bowls decorated with owls, the goddess Athena's sacred motif. Schliemann had ordered all real owls in the area to be shot, because he hated the sound of their cries ringing through the cabin at night.

Heinrich Schliemann's huge fortune meant that he had no need to raise funds to excavate. He could afford to just plough on and on.

His diaries show his lack of experience, and how confused he was by what he saw in the trenches he cut. He hadn't realized how much hard work excavating was. To his relief, he eventually found a wall, which he declared to be the "Sacred Tower of Ilium".

"Everyone must now admit," he wrote, "that I have solved a great historical puzzle." He began sending his letters from "Troy".

Schliemann's professional bacon was saved when a young Wilhelm Dörpfeld, a pioneer of stratigraphic excavation, came to him fresh from Ernst Curtius's excavations at Olympia. Like Schliemann, Dörpfeld was also obsessed with proving the truth behind Homer's epics, but his ordered and methodical approach made him much the better archaeologist.

Schliemann was prone to smuggling his finds out of the country. One early May morning, he saw the gleam of gold and copper in the ground – and declared that his workers should take *paidos*, a rest break. The find included a golden cup with the handles of a ship, decorated earrings, gold rings and bracelets, silver plus an elaborate diadem – a headdress made of 16,000 golden pieces – much of which became known as the "Jewels of Helen". He hid the treasures in his second wife Sophia's shawl, and the couple set off hot-foot to his on-site house. Overnight, fearing discovery, they moved the loot to a nearby farmhouse. Schliemann's diary entry claims that he was saving the treasure for Greece and "for archaeology". Then he promptly made off with it. The Turks, who still owned half of the site, were not pleased.

Schliemann never let the truth get in the way of a good story. He photographed Sophia in the "Jewels of Helen", and then announced that "the great Schliemann has discovered Troy!"

Or had he? Schliemann appears to have been lying. His diaries are heavily doctored. Sophia wasn't even present at the time he found "Priam's treasure" – she was in Athens, because her father was sick. A *Times* newspaper editorial even suggested that the showman had faked the jewellery and had placed it in the ground himself.

In the wet winter of 1876, Schliemann set off again, having been banned from the Turkish empire. He'd written to the Greek authorities, asking to excavate at Olympia and Mycenae, convinced that the latter was the home of the great warrior king Agamemnon. Wisely, the Greeks refused him permission.

Undaunted, Sophia and Schliemann duly turned up at Mycenae, telling the local authorities that they had a government permit. He hired a team of workers who dug for 20 days in the steaming heat before they were nearly arrested. Then the Turks stepped in. They were taking Schliemann to court for the disappearance of "Priam's treasure".

Still, Schliemann had more than enough money to get himself out of trouble. He finally got the go-ahead to excavate at Mycenae

Little remains of the glory of Troy, but new excavations in the surrounding area are revealing much about the scale of this Bronze Age powerhouse.

in 1876, although the Greek Archaeological Society kept a strict eye on him. Within a month, the team had uncovered the first of several Bronze Age chieftains. They were each buried in a "Cyclopean" tomb with spectacular weapons, wearing extraordinary gold funerary masks. This time, unable to abscond with the lot, Schliemann had to make do with the publicity. Modest as always, he announced that he had found the tombs of Agamemnon, Cassandra and Eurymedon....

Schliemann's methods were destructive and his antics illegal. Nevertheless, his dauntless spirit and compulsive storytelling inspired a whole generation to take up archaeology.

Most experts these days agree that the mound at Hissarlik was indeed Troy. Yet Schliemann's real legacy is unveiling another civilization altogether, one that we scarcely understood existed. That society was not Homeric, but Mycenaean. Schliemann and those who followed him gave us proof that advanced civilizations existed in the long-distant past during the Bronze Age.

In the 1980s, US Professor Manfred Korfmann revealed that there was a wider city of Troy. It had once extended much further out on to the plain. He also found proof in the citadel of a battle that took place in the 12th century BCE. Turkish archaeologists are still excavating the area today.

CHARLES DARWIN AND THE ORIGINS OF MAN

Encouraged by the ever more startling evidence from geologists and archaeologists, science was about to rewrite the history of life on Earth. Charles Darwin's ideas worried him so much that he confessed his concerns to his future wife, Emma Wedgwood, who urged him to read St John's Gospel. For the next 20 years, Darwin kept his more detailed conclusions to himself. Did the Theory of Evolution prove that human beings were nothing more than intelligent animals? And if humankind was the product of evolution, then what about our moral accountability to God? No less unsettling was the idea that *Homo sapiens* was not a unique creation, but one among several types of early human species. In addition, new scientific theories about glaciation raised the possibility that the Earth had experienced several Ice Ages. Thus, 1859 saw not only the publication of *On the Origin of Species*, but also the Royal Society in London published the results of decades of work by Jacques Boucher de Perthes, documenting the series of prehistoric tools he had found deep in the earth.

The Light of Knowledge

The wave of romantic nationalism that had swept Europe gave new, explosive impetus to the ideal of garnering fresh knowledge. Helped of course by a new and enlarged understanding about "deep time" and the true breadth of human history, which had been turned on their head by the theories of Darwin, archaeology began to develop a new academic rigour.

The work that had begun with small groups of amateur scholars like Stukeley, fascinated by Stonehenge, or Boucher de Perthes, obsessed with documenting the tools used by ancient man, was about to be put on a professional footing. Gradually, the practice of rich men funding their own excavations or poor men attempting to make their fortunes through treasure hunting was subsiding, as a combination of private philanthropic societies and nation states stepped in.

Sweden had appointed a chair for archaeology in the 17th century; now Leiden University in Holland appointed the world's first archaeology professor, Caspar Reuvens. In Denmark, Jens Worsaae began the fight against the "historical theory" of mythology, which held that the Old Norse myths were literally true. He argued that prehistory was a period best studied not by historians but by archaeologists, dealing with hard, material evidence, and took the Thomsen Three-Age system out into fieldwork. His layer-by-layer excavation style gradually became the standard throughout Europe – a major example of its earliest use was the excavation of Pompeii.

Inspired by the remarkable achievements of Champollion in decoding the Rosetta Stone (page 129) archaeology was, inch by inch, becoming a field of highly qualified specialists, whose methods were strikingly more methodical than their predecessors'. The pioneers included Karl Richard Lepsius who, in 1866, found the Decree of Canopus at Tanis. Written in three languages, the decree proved that Champollion's groundbreaking translation of hieroglyphics had been right.

During his travels in Egypt, Lepsius made extensive maps, plans and drawings of temples that are often the only record left. They were still being used 100 years later in 1980 to identify a "Headless Pyramid" that since Lepsius's day had been covered by a 25-ft (8-m)-high dune of sand. Lepsius, often known as the "Father of Egyptology" (although there are a number of contenders for that title), commissioned the Theinhardt font, the first hieroglyphic typeface.

Augustus Pitt Rivers, whose remarkable anthropological museum in Oxford still delights visitors today, broke the mould by visualizing his work, making it easier to understand with his highly detailed models and plans. He examined many areas of the UK, including his own estate, Cranbourne Chase, in England.

SIR WILLIAM FLINDERS PETRIE (1853–1942)

More usually known just by his last two names, Sir William Matthew Flinders Petrie was born in Charlton to the south-east of London. He was raised in a devoutly Christian home and educated at home by his parents. His father taught his son how to survey and Petrie gave his first archaeological opinion aged eight; hearing of the unearthing of the Brading Roman Villa on the Isle of Wight and the rough digging out of the villa, he asserted that the earth should be pared away, inch by inch, to see all that was in it and how it lay.

As a teenager, Petrie surveyed British prehistoric monuments to try and understand their geometry, at the age of 19 producing the most accurate survey of Stonehenge yet known. In early 1880 he travelled to Egypt to make an accurate survey of the pyramids at Giza, making him the first to fully look into their construction. His reports of the survey, and his analysis of the architecture of Giza was methodical and accurate and continues to be the basis of much of the data about the pyramids today. Even then he was horrified by how swiftly a number of monuments and mummies were being destroyed. Innovation was the order of the day in Victorian England, as was the drive for "improvement". Sir William Flinders Petrie was part of the first wave of the new professionals. He brought many useful skills that were entirely new to archaeology, including surveying, which he had been taught by his engineer father. Petrie, a brilliant mathematician, managed to refute the widespread idea that there was a "pyramid inch" by spending two years making a detailed survey of the Great Pyramid at Giza and the surrounding plain. The "inch" theory assumed that the British system of measures came from a divine and ancient source – basically inspired by the ancient Egyptians. His triangulation survey of the pyramid plateau, begun in 1880, was so accurate it is still the foundation of data used today.

Excavation is destructive. Petrie realized just how important were documentation and robust methodology. In

Khufu's Great Pyramids at Giza, centre. A mysterious new chamber has recently been discovered inside. The three smaller pyramids in front are the "Queens' Pyramids". The camels in the foreground show the massive scale.

future, people would be able to re-interpret his evidence if they needed to – especially given the number of publications he put out. Petrie and his wife Hilda went on to do work in most of Egypt's important sites, devising a new system called sequence dating. This meant adapting the Thomsen method (see pages 24–5), separation of technology types, and extending it into "typologies". Styles of pottery are used to identify stages in time.

Petrie supervised everything himself. He described Egypt as "a house on fire". Appalled at the rate of destruction he saw, he documented as much as he could, using the archaeologist's favourite new tool: photography.

In the bad old days of Egyptology, there would be a 50:50 split of finds between Egypt and the excavator. From Petrie's time onwards, Egypt, like many other states, insisted that finds remained in the country. This posed a problem in terms of funding. Petrie's private backers, like the Manchester businessman Jesse Haworth, expected a return on their investment. In the other pervading spirit of the age, a philanthropist intervened: the wealthy novelist Amelia Edwards. Edwards had become a tireless campaigner, trying to stop the destruction and neglect of Egyptian antiquity, following a trip to Abu Simbel in 1873. She co-founded the Egypt Exploration Fund, which raised independent finances for archaeology, and became Petrie's great supporter, making sure that he got an academic post at University College, London. The Fund asked him to lead a series of expeditions in Egypt and in November 1884, Petrie began his excavations, starting first with a New Kingdom site at Tanis. He swiftly took complete overall control himself, encouraging workmen to take their time with excavations to avoid damage and the overlooking of important items. In 1886 he excavated at Tell Nebesheh in the Eastern Nile Delta where he found a royal sphinx.

At the end of the Tanis dig, his funding had run out and, hoping that it would be renewed, Petrie spent 1887 cruising the Nile taking photographs. At Sehel Island near Aswan he drew and photographed thousands of early Egyptian inscriptions on a cliff face, recording embassies to Nubia, famines and wars. When his funding was renewed he went to the burial site at Fayum, where he found intact tombs and 60 portraits, learning from inscriptions that the mummies were kept with their still-living families for generations before burial. Half of the portraits were sent to the Egyptian department of antiquities, but on discovering that they were not being carefully preserved, he demanded their return. The 12 best examples were kept in Egypt, the remaining 48 sent to England for display at the British Museum. Resuming work, he discovered the village of the Pharaonic tomb-workers.

In 1890, he made the first of many trips into Palestine. His excavation of Tell el-Hesi was the first scientific excavation of an archaeological site in the Holy Land. He surveyed a group of Iron Age and early Roman tombs in Jerusalem's Wadi al-Rababah (the biblical Hinnom) and discovered that they used two different systems of measurement. In 1892, Petrie became the first Edwards Professor of Egyptian Archaeology and Philology at University College London. He continued to excavate in Egypt after taking up the professorship, training many of the best archaeologists of the day.

In early 1896, Petrie and his team were excavating a temple at Luxor, a complex just north of the original funerary temple of Amenhotep III which had been built on a flood plain. They discovered that the temple had been built by Merneptah, successor to Ramesses II, and created almost entirely from stone plundered from the temple of Amenophis III. They found a statue of Merenptah, the first known portrait of this king. Two splendid stelae, one showing Amenophis III in battle with Nubians and Syrians; the other, of black granite and more than ten feet high, was larger than any stela previously known. On its reverse was an inscription recording the triumphs of Merenptah over the Libyans and the Peoples of the Sea and, and near the end of the text a reference to another conquered people, "I.si.ri.ar" swiftly interpreted by the quick-witted Petrie as "Israel!" It was the first mention of the word "Israel" in any Egyptian text. During 1895–96, at the Ramesseum, Petrie and the young German Egyptologist Wilhelm Spiegelberg became friends. Petrie offered important collections of artefacts to the University of Strasbourg while Spiegelberg was in charge of the edition of many texts discovered by Petrie. In 1897, the Kaiser-Wilhelms-Universität Straßburg gave Petrie the title of doctor honoris causa, while in June 1902 he was elected a Fellow of the Royal Society (FRS). In 1913 Petrie sold his large collection of Egyptian antiquities to University College, London, where it is now housed in the Petrie Museum of Egyptian Archaeology. In 1922, one of his trainees, Howard Carter, went on to discover the tomb of Tutankhamun.

In 1926, the focus of Petrie's work shifted to Palestine. In 1928, he devised a new excavation system, while excavating at a vast cemetery in Luxor. The system included comparison charts for finds, a technique that is still used. He also started to work on a number of sites in the south-west of Palestine, including Tell Jemmeh and Tell el-Ajjul.

A towering figure in the history of Egyptology, Petrie's many active years led to archaeological evidence for all periods of Egyptian history from prehistory to medieval times. He worked ceaselessly to recover and document information before the pace of modern life destroyed it. His invention of sequence dating for the Predynastic period advanced chronological methods. Perhaps his most important contribution was his insistence that everything that was dug up should be recorded.

Petrie embodies the spirit of the next wave of professional archaeologists, dedicated men and women who travelled far and wide to unpick the tangled skein of world history: Alfred Kidder frantically working out a new chronology that would work for the Americas; Dorothy Garrod's revealing work in the Palaeolithic caves of Mount Carmel; Max Uhle's work in Bolivia, Peru and Chile; and Gertrude Caton Thompsen's challenge to Western assumptions about African culture. Often, their work convinced national governments to protect their most precious, if then often unrecognized, monuments. Uhle, however, still had to be supported by a rich donor: in this case, it was Phoebe Hearst, the mother of American newspaper magnate William Randolph Hearst. It was not until after World War II that institutional funding became the main commercial lifeline of the archaeologist.

Behind the Undergrowth

In the meantime, another wealthy American was about to take centre stage in the unfolding story. This romantic figure sat squarely within the adventurous tradition with which archaeology had begun, but he was no tomb raider. He also took full advantage of a new 20th-century weapon: mass publicity.

If ever a man deserves the claim to be the "real" Indiana Jones, surely it is American adventurer, aviator and academic Hiram Bingham III (see also page 84). Like his film-screen counterpart, even down to the swashbuckling hat, Bingham was both an academic (he taught history and politics at Harvard) and a dauntless traveller with a taste for adventure.

In 1911, almost delirious with the altitude, Hiram Bingham found himself high in the jungles of Peru. Below him stretched miles of verdant sub-tropical rainforest, wreathed in mist. Bingham and his small team had pushed up to 7,970 ft (2,430 m) above sea level into the Andes in search of the ruins of the last city of the Inca, Vitcos. Now, with the rapids roaring thousands of feet below, he was threading his way between great granite precipices.

All of a sudden, the American explorer came upon a starkly beautiful, towering terrace of stone, smothered with vines. They had found a lost city, a near-miracle of engineering, a palace complex that stood almost literally on top of the world: Machu Picchu.

Word of the "discovery" spread fast across the world, helped by the explorer's extraordinary ability as a publicist. Bingham always carried a camera. Unfortunately, his subsequent excavations and the rumours that surrounded them led to decades of acrimonious rhetoric. At one point in 2008, Peru even filed a lawsuit against Yale University. Finally, the parties came to terms and set up the Museo Machu Picchu at Cuzco, with most of the excavation team's finds now jointly owned.

What of Bingham's skills as an archaeologist? Bingham has had many critics – he had wrongly assumed, for example, that the site was a similar age to archaic Greece. But even now, Machu Picchu's real origins are still, like the great mountain behind it, full of mists. Research continues today.

The Spies Who Came in from the Dig

Question: Who makes the perfect spy?
Answer: An archaeologist.

Archaeologists have a perfect excuse for crossing international borders. They tend to be good at remembering detail, and have legitimate reasons to ask for access to historical archives. They often have natural opportunities to watch troop movements, or note the distribution of military hardware and bases. It would be strange if they didn't ask questions about local culture – and they can often decipher dead languages, a useful skill in mastering codes. No wonder so many archaeologists have worked for the intelligence services.

During World War I, two young men from the British Museum began to explore and survey the southern frontier of Palestine. One was Leonard Woolley, a stellar figure in 20th-century archaeology (see page 124), with many credits in the early fight to turn it into a scientific discipline. The other was a young (and also bona fide) archaeologist who had graduated from Oxford only four years earlier, Thomas Lawrence. In later life, he became known as "Lawrence of Arabia", one of the 20th century's most brilliant and fascinating military minds, credited with the invention of modern guerrilla warfare.

T. E. Lawrence was a genuine archaeologist, but then he was also a genuine spy. The mission? The so-called "Wilderness of Zin" survey. Concerned that the Ottoman Turks would join the war on the side of the Germans and Austrians, British Intelligence wanted to confirm a route for an army to cross the desert to attack at Suez, a vital strategic link between Britain and its most important colony,

India. The desert lands that lay between Palestine and the southern borders of the crumbling Ottoman empire were virtually uncharted. Lawrence had already walked 1,100 miles (1,770 km) on foot while doing his university thesis, on Crusader castles in Syria, Lebanon and Israel. His particular mission in 1911 was to monitor German progress on a railway linking Berlin with Baghdad.

Their mission sat under the cloak of the Palestine Exploration Fund, a legitimate organization specializing in biblical archaeology that still operates today. Woolley and Lawrence would excavate the site of the biblical Carchemish (Karkemish), once the eastern capital of the ancient Hittite empire, and according to the Bible, the site of the defeat of the Assyrian empire at the hands of Nebuchadnezzar, King of the Babylonians, in 605 BCE.

It was here that Lawrence learned Arabic, and began a fascination with the Middle East that was to inspire the rest of his life.

During an eventful trip to the Ile de Graye, near Aqaba, Lawrence and Woolley managed to secure the secret blueprints for the railway from a disgruntled Italian engineer. Three years later, Lawrence was commissioned into the British army and, given his specialized knowledge of the region, detailed to the British Military Intelligence Department in Cairo. He was at the head of a camel-mounted Arab army when Aqaba fell in July 1917. The famous victory was memorialized in the 1962 film *Lawrence of Arabia*.

Lawrence wasn't alone. The remarkable, pistol-packing Gertrude Bell was an invaluable resource for British Intelligence's Arab Bureau. She, too, had travelled widely in the desert, wearing a divided skirt that allowed her to ride like a man.

In 1916, Bell spied on Iraqi tribal activities around Basra. Soon, she was enlisted as the first female military intelligence officer, tasked with assessing Arab willingness to join Lawrence's anti-Ottoman revolt.

Bell was more of a cultural agent provocateur than an archaeologist per se. She helped transform attitudes to the region, and wrote the Antiquities legislation that prevented Europe's museums from simply scooping up the Middle East's entire culture. She later became the honorary Director of Antiquities for Iraq. During her many trips, she also photographed and documented hundreds of ancient and medieval structures, from Assyrian, Babylonian and Hittite archaeological sites to the minarets, mosques and palaces of early Islam.

The spying traffic wasn't all one-way. In Ireland, in the 1930s, the German director of the National Museum, Adolf Mahr, was arrested and accused of being a Nazi spy helping to plan Hitler's invasion of Ireland.

In 1917, soldiers arrested a pith-helmet-wearing American as he was about to photograph an old Spanish fort along the Honduran coast. Sylvanus Morley complained to the commanding officer: he was a specialist in Mesoamerican archaeology. He had great chutzpah: in fact the actual purpose of his trip was to hunt for German shortwave broadcast stations and submarine bases in Central America.

Morley was one of many American archaeologists and anthropologists who used their profession as cover for gathering intelligence. This patriotic willingness is perhaps not surprising. Alfred Kidder, a famous figure in American archaeology circles, served as an officer in the infantry in France; Charles Peabody taught military science. During the war, the whole top floor of the Peabody Museum at Harvard was converted to a military radio school, while part of the first floor became classrooms for the Army Training Corps. Almost the entire museum staff was involved in the war effort.

Archaeology during World War II

The advent of World War II may have put some excavations on hold, as would be the case with the survey of Sutton Hoo in the south of England, but one man remained fascinated by the secrets that archaeology could uncover.

In 1938, when Adolf Hitler paid a state visit to Rome, the Italian fascist leader Mussolini, who had once declared how much he hated German tourists brandishing guidebooks, laid on a huge welcome and an elaborate night-time motor cavalcade. The commanding beauty of ancient Rome was illuminated by 45,000 modern electric lamps, linked by 100 miles (160 km) of cabling. The Colosseum, that potent symbol of imperial power, was lit from inside by red lamps that cast a bloody glow on the grass. It fascinated Hitler.

Like many before him, Hitler drew lessons from imperial Rome, and one of those was that Rome had been a cultural cuckoo. It had greedily assimilated other influences, worshipped other nations' gods and, in so doing, turned its opponents' own soldiers against themselves. At all costs, Hitler would prepare Germany for what he saw as its destiny: creating and controlling the 1,000-year Reich.

In December 1938, a small expedition struggled slowly northwards into the Himalayas. The steep and treacherous mountain paths led them ever higher, but their 50 mules were holding up and the swastika flag still hung stiffly in the freezing air. The leader was Ernst Schäfer, like the four other scientists with him a member of the Ahnenerbe, the Nazi Ancestral Heritage Organization. At the heart of its research was the investigation of the origins and spread of the Ayran race. So what on earth were they doing in Tibet?

They were searching for the prehistoric origins of humanity. The theory seems to have sprung from the German philosopher Immanuel Kant, who labelled Tibet the birthplace of creation. He named the first, mighty race of people "Aryan" – a name derived from the Sanskrit word *arya*, meaning "noble". Mystics had later taken things further, and announced that there had once been seven "root" races in the history of humanity. One of them had first appeared on a long-lost island in the middle of the Atlantic Ocean: the legendary island of Atlantis, first described by the philosopher Plato. Survivors from Atlantis took refuge in the natural fastness of the Himalayas and established a new kingdom called Shangri-La, a Tibetan Eden. Along the way, they passed on their great knowledge and wisdom to the Aryans. This was the world's first "diffusion theory".

The party's 26-year-old anthropologist, Bruno Beger, made detailed records of the bemused locals, taking fingerprints and carefully checking facial characteristics, hair and eye colour. He became convinced that the Aryan master race was weakened after the survivors of Atlantis mixed with Tibetans. Sensing that war would soon break out and prevent them getting home, the team beat a hurried retreat after taking 2,200 photographs.

The Ahnenerbe was in the business of myth-making. The hunt for Hitler's cherished Aryans was carefully tailored to prove that the Aryans from whom the modern German race was meant to have descended had lit the first torch of civilization. The only problem was, where were Germany's magnificent, prehistoric temples? The Nazis would have to find them elsewhere....

An expedition took place to the Swedish island of Bohuslan to document petroglyphs that were, it was argued, evidence of a Bronze Age Aryan language. Himmler's Excavations department, transferred from the SS, financed 18 excavations, including many on Crete, long regarded as the potential home of the first European civilization.

Ernst Schäfer, a zoologist by training, was put in charge of excavations at Biskupin in Poland, a remarkable settlement whose fortress dates from the Iron Age. The extraordinary thing about Biskupin is that its sophisticated defences are built on an artificial island. This level of early technological innovation convinced the Ahnenerbe that the settlement must be "Aryan".

Preserved in marshland at the edge of a huge lake, the fortress was defended by a timber and earth wall 19 ft (6 m) high, and 1,500 ft (450 m) in circumference. It was constructed with parallel walls of logs, linked by cross pieces packed with clay. A belt of fir and oak poles was driven into the lake bottom at a 45-degree angle. It acted as a breakwater, an ice-breaker in the winter, and of course, provided an excellent first level of defence against attack.

The popular view is that Iron Age Europe was somehow wild and undisciplined, but Biskupin suggests otherwise: it had individual streets, public spaces, storerooms and more than 100 houses, while a wooden causeway, with a watchtower, made a link to the mainland. No wonder the Nazis wanted to lay claim to it. Modern dendrochronology of the oak used dates Biskupin's creation to the winter of 738–737 BCE.

In Germany itself, Assien Bohmers was busily digging up evidence from the Palaeolithic era, when *Homo sapiens* shared the tundra with woolly mammoths and sabre-tooth tigers.

One of the most extraordinary theories came courtesy of Walter Wurst, who believed that the warlike ancient Persians were in fact Aryans, who had supposedly lost their innate superiority due to racial intermixing. Wurst proposed an expedition to Iran to investigate the spectacular site of Naqsh-e Rustam, in the sacred mountains near Persepolis, where an inscription describes the Achaemenid emperor Darius I as an "Aryan".

While Himmler's scientists, explorers and folk historians let ideology overrule their intellectual integrity, German archaeologists were sent further afield to plunder museums and carry out illegal excavations. During the Nazi occupation of Greece, its troops used the gateway to the Acropolis as a latrine. Anti-aircraft batteries were placed inside the Parthenon, which ironically enough was itself a memorial to a devastating war.

The Fortress of the Lake

The lifespan of excavations at Biskupin in Poland neatly encapsulates the huge changes in archaeology that took place after World War II. After being abandoned, the island had gradually been reclaimed by the lake, and the anaerobic marshland had the incredible effect of preserving the wooden city.

Before the discovery of this settlement and its remarkable lake fortress, it was assumed that the prehistoric local Lusatian culture was entirely transient. In almost a century of work, archaeologists at Biskupin have learned vast amounts about this era of prehistory. In the process of tackling this huge challenge, they made many decisions that redefined archaeology for the 20th century.

Work started in 1933. It was a multi-disciplinary team, and unlike many excavations before it, came from the heart of a university. It was led by a Polish archaeologist, Professor Józef Kostrzewski of Poznan University.

Biskupin was a massive archaeological challenge, involving work in treacherous and often cold conditions, in a race against time and decay. The wet environment also meant that methods usually used in dry conditions weren't always appropriate; new field techniques had to be developed – techniques that are now applied to other wetland sites.

At first, no one realized just how quickly exposure to the open air would destroy the ancient waterlogged wood. Lots of experimentation followed, including packing the timbers with salts and trying phenolon resins. Large-scale excavation had to be halted in 1974, and today, the rest of the structure has been packed back into the earth and deluged with water.

As an academic, Professor Kostrzewski was able to co-opt diverse specialists from other areas of science into the work and open the way for archaeology to link with other disciplines, such as sociology and evolutionary ecology. Biskupin's long-lasting programme of interdisciplinary research has involved archaeo-zoologists, hydrologists, botanists, geologists, architects, palynologists, conservation experts and engineers, as well as divers from the Polish navy. This tradition has continued. Most recently, Dr Mieczysław Sinkiewicz made an extensive study into how Iron Age human occupation over generations affected the local environment.

The Biskupin site is also famous for pioneering "experiential archaeology". In sheds on site, experts recreated Iron Age technology to work out how thousands of years ago people fired pottery, baked bread and forged bronze. They also pioneered experimental breeding of Iron Age livestock: Tarpan-like horses, Red Polish cattle, heath sheep and longhorn goats.

Perhaps most importantly, Biskupin has been used to train new generations of archaeologists, en masse. Zdzisław Rajewski, who excavated after the war, set up archaeological training camps on site – the first taking place in 1951. Education programmes also raised understanding about prehistory with the general public and, today, Biskupin hosts an archaeology festival every year.

Archaeology is always massively affected by political circumstances, war being the most extreme. When the Nazis were forced to retreat, they breached the protective dykes around the site and flooded the area, hoping to destroy it. Ironically, that act of vandalism unwittingly helped to preserve the ancient timbers.

At Biskupin, here was a chance to make the past live again, and perhaps find a way of learning to live together, despite occupation and disaster. The project's directors went in for extensive reconstruction; controversial in some other countries, but certainly a positive step in helping the general public engage with history.

Biskupin has a deeper significance, however, to anyone aware of its occupied past. It is a reminder of the many insidious ways that archaeology can be made to serve the state. In Russia, archaeology had been denounced as "bourgeois" because, pre-revolution, it had always been the domain of the Tsar's court. Antiquarianism was also proscribed, as "the fetishism of objects". Biskupin, on the other hand, had no lordly halls or kingly treasure hoards. When Poland was under Soviet occupation, during 1945–89, Biskupin escaped censure because it was felt to embody an egalitarian spirit; it had been a classless home of "the people".

Nazi and Soviet occupation is just an extreme example; in interpreting archaeology, there is always the risk of contemporary cultural bias. The issue of nationalism, probably more than any other, became a concern of archaeologists post-war, prompting much intellectual angst. The archaeological record is meant to be just that: a record. A body of physical evidence about the past. Any relationship between politics and archaeologists is always going to distort the truth – whatever that turns out to be.

JÓZEF KOSTRZEWSKI (1885–1969)

Born in Węglewo in west-central Poland, Kostrzewski studied in Kraków, from 1910 onwards with the linguist and professor of archaeology, Gustaf Kossinna at Berlin, graduating in 1914. Working back in Poland he tturned Kossinna's settlement-archaeological method ("Siedlungsarchäologische Methode") on its head to try to prove that the Slavonic peoples had been native to Poland from at least the Bronze Age (the Lusatian culture) onwards. He also became involved in a war of words with the German archaeologist Bolko von Richthofen about the ethnicity of the Lusatian and Pomeranian cultures.

In 1919 he was appointed professor of prehistory at the new University of Poznań. From 1934 he was responsible for the excavation of the Iron Age settlement of Biskupin, work which continued after World War II.

During the German occupation of Poland, many universities and museums were closed, their treasures taken to Germany, and many scholars arrested, tortured and imprisoned, or killed. Kostrzewski himself hid successfully from the Gestapo during the war, returning to his academic role at Poznań in 1945.

Archaeology Comes out of the Cave

Like the human story itself, archaeology will never stand still. Over time, this ever-broadening field of study has helped us towards a much clearer understanding of the development of humanity. Taken out of the hands of the gentleman amateur, it is reinventing itself even now.

Technology is the major disruptive force today. Luckily, there is no discipline more open or more suited to the challenge of reinterpreting the evidence. As the fictional Indiana Jones says in the film *Raiders of the Lost Ark*: "Seventy per cent of archaeology is done in the library. We do not follow maps to buried treasure, and 'X' never, ever marks the spot."

Ironically, though, sophisticated digging tools and 3D detection tools are not always a good thing, at least in the wrong hands. In 2015, police in northeastern China caught 175 tomb looters, who had pillaged a Neolithic archaeological site in northeastern Liaoning province. The operation recovered 1,168 cultural relics worth more than 500 million yuan (HK$630 million). In this age of LiDAR sensors and Global Positioning Systems, it is astounding to think that there are still any archaeological sites left that could yield such riches.

Also extraordinary is the fact that the tomb of Qin Shi Huang, China's very first emperor, remains unexcavated, although the tombs of his "warriors" have been. Already, nonetheless, this multinational excavation exemplifies the technical accomplishments of professional archaeologists today. It's a world away from the unbridled, if romantic, chaos of the early 18th- and 19th-century adventurers in Egypt.

STONEHENGE: SPIRIT IN THE SKY

It's a little-known fact that Stonehenge was put up for auction in 1915. Sir Cecil Chubb bought it for £6,600 and gave it to a relieved nation. Visitor damage led to a car park being built at a distance from the henge. Unwittingly, the tarmac was laid on top of ancient wooden post-holes that have recently been carbon dated to about 6,000 years BCE – twice the age of any part of the main henge – and which are now believed to be the very first monumental structures erected in the British Isles.

The Structure

When they were first erected 4,600 years ago, the monument's vast, cut-stone sarsens would have glistened a pure, bright white. The chalk barrows and the stately ceremonial Avenue leading down to the River Avon would have shone like marble. The surrounding plain, about seven times the size of New York's Central Park, was grazed by powerful, 1.5-ton bison-like creatures, wild aurochs.

Why Stonehenge was constructed, and how, has long been a source of speculation and debate. Now, new technology is completely reshaping our understanding. The Stonehenge Hidden Landscapes Project is the world's biggest-ever "virtual" excavation to date. In five years (beginning in 2010), without excavating a thing, it created a digitized body of knowledge that would have taken decades of manual work to create.

The project has revealed up to 20 buried structures that no one has known about until now, including an extraordinary 108-ft (33-m)-long communal burial chamber dating from c4000 BCE. Thanks to this new work, archaeologists now believe that, far from being an isolated structure, this special site on Salisbury Plain formed part of a vast complex of henges, barrows and other features, all spiritually interconnected within a sacred landscape.

ROCKS OF AGES

C.4000 BCE
Date of newly discovered ceremonial burial chamber

c.3635–3570 BCE
Robin Hood's Ball

3000 BCE
First ditch built

c.2525 BCE
Durrington Walls Settlement began

2500 BCE
Inner horseshoe erected

2500 BCE
Sarsen stones erected

2400/2200 BCE
Bluestones erected

2300 BCE
Woodhenge development

2400–2200 BCE
"Amesbury Archer"

2280–1930 BCE
Re-arrangement of Bluestones

1600 BCE
Possible final arrangement of stones

The Henge's First Beginnings

One of the most exciting results of the digital survey is the previously misunderstood connection it reveals between Stonehenge and the Greater Cursus. This is an immense loop-shaped enclosure more than 1½ miles (2.5 km) long that lies north of the stones. William Stukeley imagined teams of Romans or ancient Britons racing chariots down its length, which is why he gave the feature the Latin name for a racecourse.

The Hidden Landscapes Project found two deep pits at either end of the Cursus, which probably held posts or beacons. Observed from the spot that would later become Stonehenge, the pit on the eastern side aligns with the rising sun on Midsummer's Day. The western pit aligns with its very last blink, at sunset. Stonehenge would be erected, 400 years later, at the exact point where those twin alignments intersect.

Construction

Stonehenge was built in three broad phases. The first ring ditch was dug c.5,000 years ago (i.e. c.3000 BCE) at "the dawn" of the Neolithic. Then, around 2500 BCE, huge sarsen stones were brought to the site from the Marlborough Downs many miles away and erected in a precise geometric pattern.

The inner ring of bluestones was added between 100 and 300 years later, forming a rough horseshoe inside the larger ring of sarsen stones. How these "blue" monoliths were moved from near Carn Menyn in the Preseli Hills in Wales a full 186 miles (300 km) to the west remains a matter of some debate.

The excavation in the 21st century of a nearby 2,500-year-old hill fort that was occupied in Stonehenge's later heyday led to a new analysis of a spring in the area, Blick Mead. Archaeologists had always believed the feature was part of a relatively modern 18th-century landscape garden. But a rare type of algae, *Hildenbrandia rivularis*, flourishes at Blick Mead. If you plunge a stone into the waters, expose it to the air and wait a few hours, the algae turn the stone a vivid magenta pink. Did the hunter-gatherers who first noticed the phenomenon believe there was magic at work?

New discoveries such as these all point to Stonehenge being a vibrant international centre or meeting place of some kind. Ground-penetrating radar shows that the area now known as Durrington Walls once held up to 90 standing stones and was the world's largest "super henge", some 1,640 ft (500 m) wide. Furthermore, houses in a nearby excavation appear to have been inhabited for about 50–100 years around 2500 BCE, at exactly the same time as the huge sarsen stones were being erected.

The Commercial Traveller

From its origins as a spiritual axis for ancient Britons, Stonehenge seems to have transformed into a cultural or spiritual focal point for European peoples. By the beginning of the early Bronze Age, the archaeological evidence suggests it had become a major international centre for trade that drew important and influential visitors from far and wide.

One such visitor would have been the exotic "Amesbury Archer", who lived sometime between 2400 and 2200 BCE. He takes his name from an arrowhead and two sandstone bowstring wrist guards that were found with his skeleton. A pair of gold hair ornaments also with him came from the Mediterranean. Oxygen isotope analysis of his tooth enamel reveals that he grew up in the Alps.

Temple to the ancestors? Place of healing? Astrological observatory? Trading hub? Stonehenge may be one of the most studied prehistoric places in the world, but its full story becomes more complex the more we learn. What is certain is that Stonehenge is one of the richest archaeological landscapes in the world.

Henge

The "henge" seems to be a purely British phenomenon, except for possibly the "roundel" enclosures of Bavaria's Isar Valley and Kothingeichendorf, which both have causeways very like the Avenue. These are usually found in groups, even if sometimes separated by hundreds of miles. Scholars think they were meeting places, possibly used for ritualistic purposes. In mainland Europe, there are many wooden circles of a much older date, such as the Goseck circle in central Germany, constructed c4900 BCE.

WHERE TIME STOPPED

It was 24 August 79 CE, a seemingly normal day in Pompeii in the Bay of Naples. Shortly after midday, a cracking noise split the summer air, and a menacing dark plume began to rise from the summit of nearby Mount Vesuvius. At first onlookers merely wondered at it. Then surprise turned to terror and shock. Vesuvius began shooting ash, stones and deadly fumes into the sky.

Day turned to night. Around 300 people tried to escape from the shore. Their bodies were carbonized where they stood, cowered or knelt. Fifteen miles (24 km) away, the Roman author Pliny and his family watched the disaster unfold across the bay.

In a rich seaside resort 10 miles (16 km) to the west, the catastrophe hit even harder. In Herculaneum, cascades of scorching ash and toxic gases (known as pyroclastic surges) brought the residents almost instant death. An entire world was snuffed out in a matter of minutes.

In Herculaneum, the heat actually carbonized organic substances like food, wood or leather, preserved for us to see. At Pompeii, it was different. Objects and people alike were encased in ash and lava that later hardened to a porous shell. Around 38 per cent of those who tried to flee were killed by falling roofs and collapsing walls. Two relatively ordinary places were rendered extraordinary, because of their sudden and terrible fate. Old loaves of bread sit in the oven. A mosaic "Beware of the Dog" sign is still visible in an entranceway, as are a number of political slogans for the upcoming elections.

Now the world's oldest archaeological site, it was one of the first ever to be excavated. What does it tell us? At Pompeii, in particular, life does appear to have been full of vice, at least by Victorian standards. Slavery was an accepted aspect of the daily lives of the Romans. Estimates vary, but it is thought that roughly one in three of those who lived in Italy at the time was enslaved.

However, there were also many genial aspects to life in Pompeii, not least the sumptuous fountains in the crowded streets and a well-fed way of life that was, ironically enough, helped by the fecundity of the local volcanic soil. Up until the moment of destruction, Pompeii was prosperous, and growing.

Footprints found embedded in a terracotta tile atop a temple roof demonstrate an unexpected bilingual friendship. Detfri and Amica worked in a tile factory, and perhaps did the roofing together as well. The Oscan native language works from right to left (despite being local to southern Italy). Written into the tile are the words: "Detfri, slave of Herennius Sattius, signed with a footprint." Then Amica joins her friend, writing in Latin, left to right: "Amica, slave of Herennius. Signed when we were placing the tile."

To modern archaeologists and historians, this otherwise everyday moment shows an empire still in transition. Within a century, the Oscan language would completely disappear, swallowed up by Latin. It is insights like these that make Pompeii and its archaeological legacy unique.

KARL JAKOB WEBER (1712–1764)

Born to a noble Catholic family at Arth, near Lucerne in
Switzerland, Weber was trained at the gymnasium at Lucerne,
then studied mathematics at Pavia in Lombardy. Lacking
a private income, he enlisted with a regiment of Swiss
mercenaries based in Naples. A few years later he passed the
exams for admission into the corps of military engineers, and
was accepted in the Royal Guard as an engineer in 1743. In
1749 he joined with the forces excavating the volcanically
submerged city of Herculaneum under the patronage of
Charles III of Naples.

The excavation was initially led by Roque de Alcubierre, a
Spanish military engineer who was something of a "treasure
hunter", digging out fine sculptures and other works of art
to keep his royal patron interested. Weber was later put in
charge of the excavations at Herculaneum and then Pompeii
and Stabiae. In contrast to de Alcubierre, he concentrated
on excavating whole rooms to keep everything in context, a
stance that put him at odds with his colleague.

Weber excavated the Villa dei Papiri and also recovered
much of the Theatre at Herculaneum, the Praedia of Julia
Felix on the Via dell'Abbondanza at Pompeii, for which he
drew up orthographic projections, and several villas at Stabiae,
bringing a true sense of archaeological professionalism to the
excavation of these rewarding sites. The plan he made of the
still-buried Villa of the Papyri at Herculaneum, explored room
by room by breaking through the frescoed walls, still informs
modern understanding of its layout.

People in Plaster

The 19th-century Italian excavator Giuseppe Fiorelli noticed four cavities in the layers of solidified ash in Pompeii. He realized that if he poured plaster of Paris into these voids, he could create positive copies. The first time he did this, he revealed four poignant figures: a man carrying a bag of money was leading his two small daughters, the youngest with her hair braided. Scrambling through the rubble behind them, his wife clutches a medallion of the goddess of luck.

Pompeii's cast figures are unnerving – a haunting memorial to human suffering. People are immortalized exactly as they died: a soldier who is trying to run with his long sword, a stabbing dagger and a bag of tools... A baby left in the crib in the House of the Mosaic Atrium... A man holding an axe, with which he had tried to break through a door. Perhaps the best-known cast is of a dog, fixed forever in the moment of its terror, trying to bite off its tail.

Plaster cast of a dog, caught in the throes of death.

Archaeology Gets Real

Guiseppe Fiorelli directed the Pompeii excavation from 1863 to 1875 – and hit on a better way to preserve its ruins. Before him, most of the buildings had been excavated from the side. The result was often the destruction of supporting walls and other valuable evidence. Fiorelli began uncovering the houses from the top down.

Like other archaeologists working from this period onward, he sought to employ scientific methods. Work was conducted in a systematic way, with the entire site divided into a numbered classification system of "regions", insulae (blocks) and domus (houses). He approached new areas according to a plan, rather than randomly searching for treasure. His numbering system exists in Pompeii to this day, and his methods were not just extremely influential but, in archaeological terms, invaluable.

His work showed that after the eruption, some of the luckier inhabitants actually came back: "This room has already been gone through," reads a scrawled graffito on one of Pompeii's uppermost walls.

The twin towns were entirely forgotten for more than 1,500 years. Pliny (the Younger) lost his uncle that day, and left us the only written account.

Archaeology has given the people of Pliny's time new life. One of the brightest, most delightful works of art ever found came to light only in the 1970s, in the House of the Golden Bracelet near Herculaneum. The fresco shows a glorious half-wild garden, decorated with sculptures and fountains. In it flutter beautiful wild birds: a shy golden oriole, a jay, a swallow, a magpie. It's exciting to think that there may still be many such heart-stopping frescoes waiting to be excavated.

EXCAVATION TIMELINE

1709
Theatre at Herculaneum found when a well is dug out

1735
Charles of Bourbon sends Marcello Venuti to investigate

1748
Excavations begin at Pompeii: Karl Weber develops new recording system

1860
Giuseppe Fiorelli introduces new methods

1911
Vittorio Spinazzola uses photography to record the stages of his excavation

Mosaics

Mosaic floors were made of thousands of small cubes of stone, glass or marble called tesserae. These were laid on a bed of mortar and then flattened with a wooden plank or tray to make the surface even. The tesserae were then grouted with mortar and "waxed" with a coating of olive oil. The oil enhanced the colours, as well as protecting the mosaic. Mosaics with pictorial scenes were made with the tiniest tesserae, sometimes smaller than a square centimetre. This fineness meant that the artist could vary colour, shade and line in very delicate detail. The technique is called opus vermiculatem, (literally "wormlike work"). The actual scene, usually set in the centre, was known as the emblema. Some of the world's best and biggest mosaic floors are from Pompeii, including The Battle of Issus, which shows Alexander the Great in battle. It is made with more than 4 million individual tesserae.

The Lost City?

When Hiram Bingham first saw Machu Picchu, he took the ancient citadel to be a temple to the sun, given the spiritual atmosphere of the surrounding landscape. He interpreted three unusual windows looking on to the vast mountain ranges beyond as representations of the three caves from which the mythological Inca Children of the Sun had walked into the world.

Bingham surveyed, cleared and excavated the site between 1912 and 1915, thanks to sponsorship by Yale University. *National Geographic* devoted its entire April 1913 issue to Machu Picchu and Hiram Bingham became an all-American – and then global – sensation.

Inevitably, the archaeologist overtook the site to become the story, despite efforts to keep the focus on the citadel. "We are guided solely by love and science," wrote Bingham to the *El Commercio* newspaper, "and the absolute desire to give Peru the fame it deserves."

Amid the media debate, he had his supporters. An editorial in the same newspaper argued: "Yale acts... for the benefit of Peru: it will, at its own expense, bring to life this unknown world, which has been deteriorating under the destructive action of the centuries."

Some argue that the site was a retreat, perhaps even a form of spa, for an Inca élite. Mountain or sun worship does seem a possibility. The "Inti Watana" stone was literally a "hitching post" for the sun – to lasso and keep it in its course. "Inti Mach'ay", a cave where light penetrates only for a few days in December, was the scene of a special ritual where boys watched the sun rise as they were initiated into manhood.

Machu Picchu: A Slip of the Eye

But was there ever a treasure chest? A full hundred years later, in 2011, a mountain landslide stranded French engineer David Crespy at Machu Picchu. He decided to take a longer look at the site. Not far from the entrance, he noticed an opening blocked by boulders. Crespy recorded thinking, "This is a door." The entrance was standing in plain sight, and had been seen by thousands of visitors.

The tourist reported his hunch to local Peruvian archaeologists, who promised to investigate. More than a year later, they still hadn't done anything. A frustrated Crespy contacted French historian and explorer Thierry Jamin, who had spent many years in Peru. Jamin agreed with Crespy – what lay beyond the boulders might well repay investigation.

On 19 December 2011, Jamin asked the Peruvian Ministry of Culture if his multinational team of experts could survey the space beneath the building. They would use remote-sensing, non-invasive instruments: ground-penetrating radar, an electro-magnetic resonance gun and a molecular frequency discriminator (MFD). Granted official permission, the research project went ahead in March 2012.

Almost at once, the first sensor detected a staircase, two corridors and a square central chamber. They found they could map a 3D picture of

The soaring terraces of Machu Picchu, now cleared of vines and undergrowth.

the underground complex to a depth of some 65 ft (20 m). The geo-radar also revealed several smaller rooms and a series of cavities that looked as if they might be graves.

The team swept the subterranean complex with the instruments again. The results were even more astonishing. The steps leading down to the central chamber were made of gold. Had they discovered the mausoleum of Pachacutec? The sensors showed there were more gold and silver objects inside.

On 22 May 2012, Jamin asked the Ministry of Culture if he and his team could remove the giant boulders blocking access to the subterranean complex and investigate it in person. In November 2012, with local officials criticizing what they described as the project's "lack of scientific methodology", Peru's Directorate General of Cultural Heritage turned him down. The Ministry of Culture and Machu Picchu's directors also said they were worried that any excavation could jeopardize the stability of the site, a concern others dismissed.

One thing is for certain: if the Peruvian authorities ever do allow an archaeological team to investigate and they find the Inca equivalent of King Tut's tomb, then the number of tourists wishing to visit Machu Picchu will explode.

HIRAM BINGHAM III (1875–1956)

Bingham was born in Honolulu, Hawaii and educated at O'ahu College and Phillips Academy in Andover, Massachusetts. He gained degrees from Yale, the University of California, and a PhD from Harvard. He taught history and politics at Harvard and at Princeton, in 1907 was appointed as a lecturer in South American history and became a pioneer of teaching and research on Latin American history in the US, publishing an assessment of how the subject might develop in 1908.

Although not a trained archaeologist, it was during his time at Yale that Bingham rediscovered the largely forgotten Inca city of Machu Picchu. In 1908 he attended the First Pan American Scientific Congress at Santiago, Chile. Making his way home via Peru, a local official suggested that he visit the pre-Columbian city of Choquequirao which he wrote about in *Across South America*; an account of a journey from Buenos Aires to Lima by way of Potosí, with notes on Brazil, Argentina, Bolivia, Chile, and Peru.

The visit caught Bingham's imagination and in 1911 he organized the Yale Peruvian Expedition, an objective of which was to search for the last capital of the Incas. With help from local people, he identified both Vitcos and Vilcabamba, which he named "Eromboni Pampa". He failed to recognize Vilcabamba as the last capital, identifying Machu Picchu as the "Lost City of the Incas", an oversight not corrected until many years later by the Andean explorer Vince Lee.

On 24 July 1911, a man named Melchor Arteaga took Bingham to Machu Picchu. With the support of Yale and the National Geographic Society Bingham returned to Peru in 1912, 1914 and 1915. His book *The Lost City of the Incas* (1948) explains how he came to believe that Machu Picchu was the site of a major religious shrine and a training centre for religious leaders, although subsequent research suggested that it was a royal estate used by Inca leaders and their entourage in the height of summer.

Tall, lean and handsome, Bingham was lucky enough to marry the granddaughter of the jeweller Charles L. Tiffany, whose wealth was one reason that the academic could afford to travel more or less at whim. He has been cited as one possible basis for the character Indiana Jones.

Bingham achieved the rank of captain of the Connecticut National Guard in 1916. In 1917, he became an aviator and organized the United States Schools of Military Aeronautics at eight universities to provide ground school training for aviation cadets. He served the Aviation Section, U.S. Signal

Corps and the Air Service, attaining the rank of lieutenant colonel. In Issoudun, France, Bingham commanded the Third Aviation Instruction Center, the Air Service's largest primary instruction and pursuit training school. He became a supporter of the Air Service in their post-war quest for independence from the army and supported that effort, in part, with the publication of his wartime experiences titled *An Explorer in the Air Service* published in 1920 by Yale University Press.

During the 1920s, Bingham entered politics, first as lieutenant governor, then in 1924 governor of Connecticut. In 1924 he was elected as a Republican in the US Senate. He only served as governor for one day. Though re-elected to a full Senate term in 1926 his term was not without controversy and he lost his seat in the Democratic landslide of 1932 that followed the Great Depression.

During World War II, Bingham lectured at several United States Navy training schools. In 1951 he was appointed chairman of the Civil Service Commission Loyalty Review Board, an assignment he kept through 1953.

Machu Picchu has become a leading tourist attraction in South America with Bingham acknowledged as the man who brought it to the attention of the world. The precarious road that takes tourists to the site is now called the Hiram Bingham Highway.

Popularity

Machu Picchu's immense popularity is today threatening to overwhelm both it and the local region. The Peruvian authorities have now limited visitor numbers to 2,500 a day. Nevertheless, they allowed the construction of a luxury hotel very close to the entrance. Mass tourism and associated development is undermining the natural habitat of animals like the "Spectacled" or Andean Short-faced bear, the model for the much-loved children's story character Paddington Bear. Archaeological exploration brings wonders to light – but is our desire to visit sites like Machu Picchu in large numbers a good thing?

CHINA: THE TERRACOTTA ARMY

In 1974, a group of Chinese fruit farmers made one of the world's most unexpected discoveries. The area around Mount Li, near the city of Xi'an in Shanxi province, was suffering from a severe drought. Desperate for water for their produce, Yang Quanyi and his five friends decided to dig a well under their persimmon orchard. Quanyi recalled: "Suddenly, I hit the stone man's neck. I told my friend: 'This is a hidden temple.'" His first thought was almost right.

The scale of the "Terracotta Army", as it is popularly known, is almost impossible to convey. Rows of lifelike statues extend as far as the eye can see, yet only a small proportion have as yet been excavated.

Inside was a dazzling spectacle: a life-size army of painted clay soldiers that had lain underground for 2,200 years. The massed ranks of terracotta warriors constitute one of the most astonishing finds in the history of archaeology, but form only a tiny part of a long-buried mausoleum built for China's very first emperor, Qin Shi Huang.

There was no record of this burial in existence: no paintings, no stories, not even any local myths. The farmers were astonished. Yet the complex built by the conqueror and war leader who gave his name to the country we know today (Qin is pronounced "Chin") covers an area of 35 miles^2 (90.6 km^2).

When Qin came to the throne as a boy in 246 BCE, he ruled a small and not especially powerful state surrounded by many hostile rivals. By 221 BCE, he had conquered not just its closest and most persistent enemy, Chu, but all of the land that we now know as China.

The Qin emperor's grandiose ambitions extended beyond the mortal realm. Believing he could cheat death, he created a subterranean pleasure and fortress complex. It was laid out in beautiful grounds, perhaps an idealized and enhanced version of the extraordinary world he had enjoyed as sovereign. Among the numerous highlights of his vision for the afterlife are twin half-sized chariots embellished with gold and silver – each pulled by a team of four magnificent terracotta horses – and performing troupes of musicians and acrobats.

The Pits

The clay figures so far discovered lie buried in three pits, just under 1 mile (1.5 km) to the east of the tomb. Some may even be genuine likenesses of the real soldiers who had helped him conquer so much in the span of his 37-year reign. The figure-makers clearly strived for realism. The detail recorded on the thousands of figures, vehicles, animals and equipment in the pits is astonishing – and gives us an unparalleled insight into a vanished empire.

To date, more than 1,100 figures have been restored and now stand vigil in Pit One – but surveys show that more than 6,000 warriors are buried here, with a further 2,000 in Pits Two and Three. Armed with specially produced spears, halberds and swords, even today they are a fearsome and awe-inspiring sight. The power and accuracy of their crossbows in particular would not be matched in Europe for another 2,000 years. Shen Maosheng, head of the archaeological team, plans to make precise models

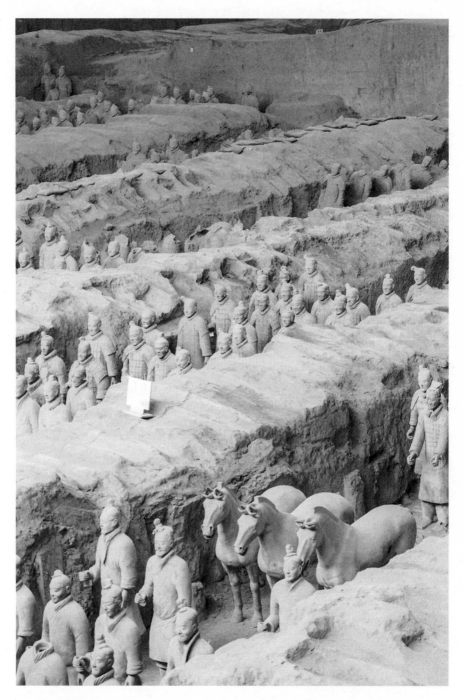

The scale of the "Terracotta Army", as it is popularly known, is almost impossible to convey. Rows of lifelike statues extend as far as the eye can see, yet only a small proportion have as yet been excavated.

to help work out their shooting range more accurately. Researchers are using a novel technique to establish both how the weapons were produced, and how effective they were. The substrate used to make dental moulds is being applied to the metal surfaces, and the resulting highly detailed impressions are examined under a scanning electron microscope. In this way, no harm is done to the actual objects.

The warriors were ranged in Qin battle formation, with the archers in the vanguard and on the flanks protecting a core of heavy infantry and chariots. The researchers are using a pioneering technique known as, X-ray fluorescence (XRF) spectrometry, to find out what the crossbow bolts were made from. XRF can typically analyse elements from sodium to uranium, and is revolutionizing the way in which archaeologists are able to do their work.

Along with the armies of warriors, the pits contain terracotta models of scribes and scholars, acrobats, musicians and weightlifters. Digs at what were plainly intended to represent outlying gardens have turned up dozens of sculpted waterfowl and birds. Everywhere, there are the stocky brown horses that must have played a key role in Qin-era life.

Most of the huge area is still unexcavated, and archaeologists are keenly aware that subsequent discoveries may change both their view of what they have already found and their view of Qin civilization as a whole.

Archaeology Today

Nowadays, archaeology is a complex business, involving teams consisting of experts in a diverse range of subjects. But all archaeologists have to begin at the same point: they need to find a place to investigate.

Finding a Site

When the crime writer Agatha Christie married archaeologist Max Mallowan in the 1930s, she described walking across hundreds of "tells" in Syria, to try to find the best mound to excavate. They walked so much that her shoes wore out.

Today, archaeologists can employ a variety of technologies to help them pinpoint a likely site for a dig. These can involve everything from metal detectors to satellite imagery.

Discovering an Archaeological Site

There are various ways that a potential site for excavation can be discovered. They include:

- Farmers often make discoveries when ploughing fields
- Construction crews laying foundations or creating tunnels
- Old documents or histories suggesting previous human occupation
- Aerial or satellite surveys
- Local knowledge

Technological Developments

Technology is fast transforming archaeology. The discipline is now situated somewhere between the hard, natural sciences, historical studies and the social sciences. Archaeologists are still highly fond of the trowel, but they are also embracing new digital technologies that include:

1. **X-ray Fluorescent Spectrometry (XFS):** A pioneering technique originally developed for the engineering industry, the latest hand-held device provides a detailed chemical analysis of most materials, including metals, glass and ceramics.

2. **Ground-Penetrating Radar (GPR):** GPR works by transmitting tiny pulses of energy into a material and recording the strength and the time required for the return of any reflected signal. A series of pulses over a single area make up a scan.

3. **Electromagnetic Induction (EM):** In its simplest form, EM measures the change in impedance between a transmitter coil and a receiver coil when the magnetic field they generate encounters a conductive material – e.g. a copper object – in the ground. The receiver senses the type and distribution of the material, and

identifies it by measuring the induced secondary magnetic field.

4. **Molecular Frequency Discriminator (MFD):** All elements have a unique "molecular resonant frequency". Gold, for example, resonates at 5 KHz, and silver at 8.7 KHz. The MFD's small transmitter unit generates the frequency that matches the frequency of the target substance.

5. **Software and Photography:** Chinese researchers working with University College London have found a cheap way to create 3D images of objects – in this case, of the heads of famous Chinese warriors in the Terracotta Army – by taking multiple photographs of each one, and using a "sparse point cloud" software process to map individual details.

6. **Remote Sensing from Space:** Near-infrared satellite imagery sweeps the Earth's surface from space, reflecting parts of the electromagnetic spectrum that are invisible to the human eye. The otherwise undetectable changes in surface density are then colour-coded by special software. The technology reveals long-hidden patterns and shapes in the landscape and can direct archaeologists to promising excavation sites.

7. **Airborne LiDAR (Light Detection and Ranging):** LiDAR employs an airborne laser to measure the exact distance between the scanning equipment and the ground. Multiple laser pulses produce high-definition digital elevation models (DEMs) of the landscape below, which can then be modified and viewed from any angle. It is able to detect height differences of no more than a few centimetres in ground level variations, revealing sites that have lain undetected for centuries.

8. **Accelerator Mass Spectrometry (AMS):** AMS radiocarbon dating allows archaeologists to obtain dates from samples that are very much smaller than those needed for standard radiocarbon

dating. The accelerator-based mass spectrometer counts all of the C14 atoms, rather than just those atoms that are decaying as happens in the standard process, making AMS dates more precise, although it is currently a very expensive process. AMS is also used to count isotopes. In the late 1980s, archaeologist Douglas Price and geochemist Jim Burton developed a new technique that measured the ratio of strontium isotopes in human bones. It acts as a chemical signature of the local geology within the body.

9. **Dual energy (Computed Tomography) CT scan/X-ray Visualization:** A CT scanner is a special X-ray machine that takes a series of detailed images of a body. Among other things, the dual CT process can help experts determine what people ate, and what types of disease, if any, they suffered.

Digging the Dirt

Archaeological sites can be difficult to read, unless they are approached with a combination of two things: knowledge and imagination. What looks to the untrained eye like a pile of stones could actually be the entire water system of a Roman building. Once you've found something, how do you date it?

We tend not to give soil a second's thought, but along with water and oxygen, it is what sets Earth apart from other planets. Dirt didn't make its first appearance until 450 million years ago – even though the Earth itself is 4.54 billion years old.

Intimate contact with dirt goes hand in hand with archaeology. To those in the know, soil is like a visible map of time. Lasagne-like, it exists in layers, one built on top of another. There are two aspects to this: the first is stratification, and the second is the geological law of superposition. Steno's law holds that the oldest layers of earth are those that are closest to the centre of the earth.

Stratification: Natural processes cause the layering of soils – a river eroding its banks and then depositing a layer of silt, for instance. But even without the action of rivers, it is surprising how much matter can build up at an abandoned place. Structures decay, crumble and gradually return to the land. Water, wind and gravity carry soil from high or exposed regions to deposit it in more sheltered areas. As this soil mixes with leaf and plant mould, and the whole process starts over again.

Sometimes, geological strata can be confusing. Erosion, rodent burrows, or posts driven into the soil can make the stratigraphy much more difficult to read because they disturb the original, natural layers. For archaeologists, however, these intrusions are important, as they are often the product of human behaviour.

Stratigraphy creates a context, a framework of time and space that is everything to an archaeologist. Once a shard of pottery or a fragment of jewellery is out of the ground, its context is lost. The archaeologist's goal is to detect and record the web of information between an object and its context that allows them to reconstruct a chain of events. In other words, not just what happened, but how and why it happened.

Over the 250 years that archaeologists have been recording and dating, they have created intricate "typologies" for objects such as pottery and stone tools that change in style over the centuries and help date specific layers. This is known as "relative" dating.

So how to record all this information? There is a universal system for documenting site stratigraphy with a visual cross-section, called the Harris Matrix. Dr Edward Harris came up with it in the 1970s when working on a large-scale, urban site in the English city of Winchester. He wanted to record the material clearly, in ways that future excavators could understand. These days the original layers and positions of finds and samples are also measured, digitized and registered in GIS-programmes, and can even be rendered in 3D, but they are still using this basic conceptual technique.

The Human Factor: There are both "naturally" and "culturally" created soil layers, and as you'd expect, towns and cities have their own complications, called human beings. They themselves add to the accumulating layers, and the picture can be quite confusing.

To make the archaeological picture more complicated, people also burn, abandon or tear down the buildings their ancestors built. They then build on top of the ruins, making urban sites much more complex than rural ones.

Garbage, or anything that people no longer have a use for, eventually, through the action of earthworms, water and microbial activity, turns into carbon-rich soil. Stuff breaks down as geological and biological remains mix with the archaeological traces of houses and streets as well as artefacts like pot sherds or old clay pipes. In addition, the older the city, the higher the modern ground level is likely to be.

In the past 100 years, the world population has exploded. Today, through mining activities alone, *Homo sapiens* moves more sediment than all the world's rivers combined. One wonders what types of "stratigraphy" will confront the archaeologists of the future.

Forensic Evidence

It's easy to see why "Forensic" archaeology has become a specialist area. Modern, non-invasive technologies developed in archaeology save time, money and a huge amount of effort when surveying large areas of ground. In the 21st century, advanced Bluetooth technologies developed for land surveying can plot grid coordinates, record distance, and compute angles of elevation on hillsides. Then, the captured data can be entered into a 3D mapping programme that runs on a laptop.

- **Skeletal Analysis:** To work specifically in skeletal analysis you need advanced training in osteology, or skeletal anatomy and biology. Skeletal remains are also very important when it comes to understanding the very distant past: our human origins. Skeletal remains give unique insights into an individual. They can tell us about the society that person lived in, their status, religion, diet or illnesses. Depending on age, there are between 206 and 270 bones in the human body, all of which have to be recorded, examined and packed away on any excavation. It's the job of the archaeologist not only to identify what they see, but also to record everything. Particularly wet, arid or frozen environments can stop even soft tissue from deteriorating. Bodies deep-frozen soon after death can survive remarkably well, the most famous example being "Ötzi the Iceman", who lived around 3300 BCE.

- **Reading the Bones:** Where do you start? – Many human remains, like Kennewick Man, are found by accident. Archaeologists are often called in to investigate ahead of building development work to prevent this kind of unexpected discovery. The process is sometimes called "rescue" or "salvage" archaeology. How do archaeologists identify what they see?

- **Age**: The most basic question to ask is: are we dealing with a child or an adult? Overall size obviously defines very young children, as does wrist size. Part of a child's skull is open, to allow room for growth. The better fused and smoother the skull, the older the individual was at time of death. From the age of about 13 years, different bones fuse at different ages. A complicating factor is that malnutrition delays this process. Ageing a skeleton is more difficult in adults, once all the bones have fused. There are agreed scientific formulas that can help estimate height, based on the length of leg and arm bones. Beyond the age of 12 years, height stops being a reliable way to distinguish a child from an adult. The developmental stage of the teeth is one of the best guides. The first permanent molar erupts at the age of six years, the second at the age of 12, and the third at c.18–21 years. Tooth wear is another indicator of age, but varies immensely with different diets. Sometimes the best that can be done is to place skeletons into simple age categories – young, middle-aged or old.

- **Sex:** Although adults are easier to deal with than children, humans are still endlessly variable. There is not always a clear difference between a small man and a large woman, even in terms of hand size. The most significant biological difference between men and women is the pelvis. Males tend to have a narrower and deeper sciatic notch. A man's pelvis is long and narrow; a female pelvis tends to be wider and bowl-shaped. The next best indicator is the skull. Brow ridges are smaller in women and there may also be subtle differences in the shape of the eye sockets.

- **Height:** Archaeology is about analysis, gradually building data sets by making and recording detailed measurements. These patterns sometimes yield unexpected results. Over years of study it became clear that in Roman Britain the average height of a man was around 5 ft 7 in (1.65 m) while men across the rest of the Roman empire were taller than Britons. This became important when in 2005, archaeologists discovered a gladiator cemetery outside York. The first clue that these were gladiators was that all the skeletons were exceptionally tall.

- **Disease:** Ancient afflictions, trauma or congenital disease do show up in bones. Various types of records including historical documents, medical instruments and of course art can tell us about the illnesses people have suffered from. Not many infections reach the bone. Acute diseases such as the plague and smallpox tend to kill or be cured very quickly and do not have time to affect the skeleton; nor do diseases such as measles, smallpox, plague and flu, although tuberculosis does. Congenital diseases are the most common diseases found in skeletal material. They include osteoarthritis, osteoporosis, and general changes associated with the ageing process.

- **Nutrition:** Radiography, CT scanning, microscopic analysis and DNA analysis can all reveal information about diet and health. Iron deficiency anaemia, vitamin D deficiency and the haemorrhaging that comes with scurvy all show up on bones.

- **Teeth:** Through teeth, archaeology gives us a long-term view of human health. There was a time when museum curators carefully cleaned up their exhibits. Not any more: thanks to the dental calculus, or mineralized dental plaque on their teeth, we now realize that Neanderthals weren't entirely carnivorous, as was once assumed. They ate a mixed diet and even turned to plants for pain relief.

- **Circulatory problems:** If the blood supply to an area of bone is cut off, that area of the skeleton will die and may be reabsorbed. Osteochondritis dissecans is a relatively common disease which falls into this category and tends to be associated with physical trauma.

What does it take to preserve a human bone?

The greatest enemies of preservation are water, air and variable temperatures. Sand preserves bone very well if it's dry, whereas salt and chalk are more destructive. An acidic environment attacks the mineral components of a skeleton. A good example is the remarkable Anglo-Saxon burial at Sutton Hoo in the east of England, where the sandy soil is generally pH 3–4. Where once lay the body of a mighty king, nothing was left in the ground bar a greenish stain. The best-preserved human remains tend to come from places with extreme climates. On high, dry mountaintops bodies can even be found freeze-dried. The high Chilean Andes, arid areas such as Egypt, the Sudan and the north-west of China can yield near-perfect mummies. In ancient Egypt, the practice of mummification helped to preserve the dead and has been extensively researched.

Carbon Dating

Carbon is everywhere: in the atmosphere, in the earth and in the oceans. The invention of radiocarbon dating has changed the way we see the oceans, rocks and soils of Earth. It has also given us completely new insights about human history.

There are two main methods of dating archaeological finds. "Relative" dating means working by association: studying the types of tools or pottery finds and comparing them with others from the same culture. This is called seriation. The other method is called "Absolute" dating. This is a misnomer, as even high-technology techniques are not exactly "absolute", making more of a reasonable approximation.

There are a number of "Absolute" techniques, but it was radiocarbon dating that caused the revolution. The process can determine the age of anything from an Egyptian mummy to a prehistoric poppy. Its inventor, American chemist Willard Libby, won a Nobel prize for his invention, just in time to help authenticate some of the most controversial documents in the world: the Dead Sea scrolls.

- **Carbon-14/Radiocarbon**: Carbon-14 is the ticking clock inside each and every one of us. Also known as radiocarbon, it is generated in the upper atmosphere and enters our bodies through natural processes like breathing, or eating the plants that themselves take in carbon to grow.

  There are three types of carbon isotope: Carbon-12, Carbon-13 and Carbon-14. Unlike 12 and 13, the radioactive isotope Carbon-14 is highly unstable. When a creature dies, the radiocarbon begins to decay. The rate of its decay can be measured and compared with the levels of other carbon atoms. That ratio establishes a chronology for any once-living organism. Its usual range is up to 30,000 years, but with sensitive (and expensive) instruments, it's possible to push this further, possibly even up to 70,000 years.

  Libby initially calibrated his "clock" by dating objects of known age such as Egyptian mummies and bread from Pompeii. Today, it is measured against the known ages of tree rings. As a rule, carbon dates are younger than calendar dates: 20,000 carbon years roughly equates to 24,000 calendar years.

  The new dating technique has changed our approach to archaeology itself. The very fact it exists has made it possible to take a broader look at human prehistory. Combined with the astonishing advances in DNA science, we are now able to begin rewriting the entire map of human life on Earth.

- **Difficulties with Dating:** The amount of Carbon-14 in the atmosphere fluctuates, affected by cosmic radiation and factors on Earth such as volcanoes or sudden upsurges in pollution, both of which belch carbon into the air. Nuclear tests in the 1950s and 1960s had a big impact on Carbon-14 levels in the world's atmosphere. In the early days of radiocarbon dating, this was a problem. A huge amount of work has gone on since then to create an internationally agreed, historical "calibration" curve that takes changing carbon levels into account.

WHAT CAN BE CARBON DATED?

Radiocarbon dating only works on organic materials, and then only if they haven't mineralized. Neither stone nor metal can be tested. So what can be?
- Plant matter, seeds, spores and pollen
- Peat, mud and soil
- Bones, hair and blood
- Paper or parchment
- Leather or fur
- Shells, coral or chitin
- Wall paintings (the substances used to make the paint)
- Wood or charcoal

The Origins of Humankind

In the 1800s, most people believed the Earth was about 6,000 years old, because of the accounts written in the Bible about the Creation. Archaeology was about to unravel these assumptions. In 1856, in the serene Neander Valley in Germany, workers quarrying for limestone dug out heavy bones like those of a bear and a strange, human-like skull. A local schoolteacher, Johann Carl Fuhlrott, had to save them from the spoil heap. The skull had a prominent brow and deep eye sockets.

A keen amateur naturalist, Fuhlrott turned to the Professor of Anatomy at the University of Bonn, Hermann Schaaffhausen. He was convinced that they belonged to a "savage and barbarous" race of humans. It soon emerged that other bones like these were being found across Europe. Together they announced the discovery publicly in 1857. In their view the bones represented the remnants of an ancient human race, different from contemporary humans.

Their views were not readily accepted as they contradicted literal interpretations of the Bible, and Charles Darwin's work about evolution had not yet been published.

The discovery of Neanderthals, a human-like species that was nevertheless not human, became a key piece of evidence supporting the direct evolutionary link between modern humans and apes. *Homo sapiens* was not unique after all, but merely one of several types of early human species. Over the following years, further evidence of human ancestors continued to emerge.

Johann Carl Fuhlrott, who set in motion the identification of Neanderthals.

A skull of Homo neanderthalensis, 30,000–50,000 years old.

THE ANCESTORS OF HUMANITY	c.4.5 million years ago–2 million years ago
	Australopithecus
	2.4 million years ago–1.4 million years ago
	Homo habilis
	1.9 million years ago–143,000 years ago
	Homo erectus
	600,000–200,000 years ago
	Homo heidelbergensis
	400,000 years ago–c.40,000 years ago
	Homo neanderthaleris
	c.200,000 years ago–present
	Homo sapiens

Lucy and Naia

In 1974, the American anthropologist Donald Johanson discovered the skeleton of "Lucy" in Ethiopia, an *Australopithecus afarensis*, a precursor species to humanity that had lived 3.2 million years ago.

Once modern humans evolved, they gradually spread across the globe. From their origins in Africa, they first moved into southern Asia and Europe, and from there expanded into Australasia, Polynesia and the Americas. There were two waves of migration, the first through North Africa 130,000–115,000 years ago and the second following the southern coast of Asia 77,000–69,000 years ago.

"Naia", named after the water nymphs of mythology, is one of the oldest and most complete human skeletons discovered in the Americas. The body was found wholly by chance, in waters 140 ft (42.6 m) below water in a spectacular cave in Mexico's Yucatán peninsula. On an expedition funded by *National Geographic*, Mexican divers Alberto Nava Alejandro Alvarez and Franco Attolini explored

The skeleton of Lucy (*Australopithecus afarensis*), displayed in the Natural History Museum of Vienna.

an immense underwater crevasse they called Hoyo Negro, the "black hole". There, they saw the remains of a teenage girl who had died 13,000 years ago; the young woman's body was found lying on a small ledge.

Naia's skeleton was left surprisingly intact. Amazingly, it was still possible to extract DNA from her teeth, and for experts studying her skull to reconstruct her facial features. When her DNA was studied by Mexico's National Institute of Anthropology and History, it shed fresh light on a big controversy: who were the first Americans, and how did they arrive in the western hemisphere? Her DNA, with clear links to modern Native Americans, strengthened the evidence for the Bering Land Bridge theory.

Stone Age Cultures

In the 18th century scholars began to notice evidence of human activity – stone tools like axes, hammers, flints and arrowheads – buried deep in the ground. The realization was a key moment in the development of stratigraphy.

In East Africa, palaeontologists have found many sophisticated tools that pre-date the emergence of *Homo sapiens*. Other hominids could make tools. In 1929, the Kenyan Louis Leakey visited Olduvai Gorge in Tanzania in search of fossils, but found some of the earliest hand-made tools ever discovered. The site held more than 2,000 stone tools including hand-axes, scrapers and stitching awls. With his wife, Mary, he began studying an unimaginably ancient time.

The finds dated back to approximately 1.8 million years ago – before modern humans had even evolved. Further research by Sonia Harmand and Jason Lewis in 2011 uncovered even older tools. They found 20 artefacts at the Lomekwi site in Kenya dating back 3.3 million years: the first known material evidence of human history.

A hand-axe from Olduvai Gorge, over a million
years old, now in the British Museum.

In the Upper Palaeolithic, approximately 40,000 years ago, a
revolution took place. The crude tools of the past were replaced
with far more complex technologies, social structures and cultural
practices. Bows and spears were invented to make hunting easier.
Art, ritual and religion began to emerge. Artwork has been found
at caves at Lascaux, Cosquer Cave and Chauvet Cave in France,
ranging in age from 30,000 to 17,000 years ago.

It was not only in Africa that prehistoric bones upset ideas
on human development. The "Red Lady of Paviland" may have
revealed intricate burial practices on the part of our early hunter-
gatherer forebears, but a vast pit at Sima de los Huesas in Spain
showed that some hominids buried their dead in mass graves. These
earliest-known residents of Europe lived between 1.2 million and
600,000 years ago.

OLDUVAI GORGE

Louis and Mary Leakey started their research at Olduvai Gorge in 1951 followed by a more extensive excavation in 1952. They found evidence of a prehistoric bog where a variety of animals had been trapped, slaughtered and butchered.

In 1959, further excavations took place, and while Louis was unwell, Mary discovered a fossilized skull which was given the number OH 5. It was *Paranthropus boisei*, called "Zinjanthropus" or "Zinj". Did the fossil belonged to *Paranthropus*, a genus discovered earlier by Robert Broom, or was it a member of a different genus, that was ancestral to humans? Louis opted for *Zinjanthropus*, a decision that attracted the attention of Melville Bell Grosvenor, president of the National Geographic Society whose interest in the find led to an article in *National Geographic* and, more importantly, a large grant to continue work at Olduvai. The dating, in 1960 of Bed I of the site to almost 1.89 million years ago at its oldest confirmed the extreme antiquity of fossil hominids found in Africa.

When, in 1960, Mary became director of excavation at Olduvai, she set up Camp 5 and employed a number of Kamba assistants, including Kamoya Kimeu – the man who later found a large number of east Africa's most famous fossils.

At a site known as "Jonny's site", Mary and Louis' son Jonathan found two skull fragments that Mary linked to *Telanthropus*, a partial skull found by Robert Broom and John T Robinson in 1949, later designated as an example of *Homo erectus*. A short while later Louis, his son Philip and Ray Pickering found a fossil Louis designated as "Chellean

Man", as a result of the Oldowan tools found nearby. After reconstruction Louis and Mary named the skull "Pinhead" and it was later identified as *Homo erectus*, the same age as *Paranthropus* at 1.4 million years old.

In 1962 Louis was visiting Olduvai when Ndibo Mbuika discovered the first tooth of *Homo habilis*. Initially Louis and Mary believed it to be female and named her Cinderella, or Cindy. The South African palaeoanthropologist Phillip Tobias identified Jonny's Child, a fragmented lower mandible alongside it while Raymond Dart came up with the name *Homo habilis*. This fossil was regarded as an intermediate stage between the gracile (or slender) *Australopithecus* species (*afarensis* and *africanus*) and *Homo*, the precursors to *Homo sapiens*.

JOHN FRERE'S "WEAPONS OF WAR"

In 1797, the English antiquary John Frere found ancient artefacts deep in the ground while digging in a clay pit in Suffolk. He was sure they were weapons, but they were under sand and embedded underneath 12 ft (4 m) of undisturbed soil. The sand layer also held shells and the remains of tiny marine creatures. How could any "weapons of war", which must have been made by man, have at one stage been beneath the sea? John Frere's "weapons of war" were later recognized as Acheulean hand-axes, so named after the archaeological site in France where the tools were first identified, St Acheul.

THE LASCAUX CAVES

In the village of Montignac in southwestern France, a local teenage boy, Marcel Ravidat, and three of his friends, armed with only a lamp to guide their way, ventured into a deep cave searching for treasure. They found a treasure of an entirely different sort – the walls were covered with prehistoric paintings. These depict animal and human figures, using ochre and other mineral pigments. In 1950, the paintings at Lascaux were Carbon-14 dated at 17,000 years old. It is not just the paintings that fascinate experts: there are almost 1,500 engravings, several signs and holes in the wall that indicate prehistoric scaffolding used to create the paintings. Visitor numbers over the years threatened Lascaux and, as a result, even older cave art (discovered by potholers in 1994) at Chauvet Cave, in the Ardèche Gorge in southern France, can be viewed only in replica form, at a major new visitor centre which documents a full 50,000 years of dramatic cave art in the region.

THE "RED LADY OF PAVILAND"

The Paviland Cave in South Wales is a lonely place, accessible only at low tide and requiring a sheer climb to reach it. Thirty-five thousand years ago, a group of hunter-gatherers hauled a body up the steep slope to this magnificent position. At that time, sea levels were much lower and the cave looked out over a 70-mile (115-km)-wide plain teeming with wildlife. As they laid him to rest, the group smeared the body with red ochre, decorated it with painted shells and surrounded it with ivory – showing extraordinary commitment to someone who must have been very important. The remains were first discovered and named in 1823 by the Reverend William Buckland, an eccentric Professor of Geology at Oxford University. On 18 January 1823 Buckland entered Paviland Cave, where he discovered a skeleton which he named the "Red Lady of Paviland", believing it to be the bones of a local prostitute. In fact, it was the body of the oldest anatomically modern human ever discovered in the United Kingdom. The skeleton was found in same strata as the bones of extinct mammals (including mammoth). Buckland shared the view of French naturalist Georges Cuvier that humans had not existed at the same time as any extinct animals. Because of this he believed that the grave was historical but not ancient, perhaps dating from the same period as some nearby pre-Roman fortifications. Carbon-dating has since suggested that the skeleton is around 33,000 years old.

Cradles of
Civilization

The Fertile Crescent

About 9 miles (15 km) from the city of Sanliurfa in Turkey is the oldest sacred temple ever discovered in the world: Göbekli Tepe. It dates back 12,000 years. The extraordinary finds at this site have forced us to rewrite the story of human history. A civilization capable of advanced architecture and symbolic art is not supposed to have existed so long ago.

From 3500 BCE onwards, a series of developed city-states began to appear in Sumer, the fertile area of Mesopotamia between the Tigris and the Euphrates rivers. This is the first place that writing was invented, in pictographs and then cuneiform script, and also where the world's earliest cities developed.

Historians have often called the Middle East "the cradle of civilization". In particular, they refer to the Fertile Crescent – a wide sweep of land that reaches from the Persian Gulf to present-day Lebanon, Israel, Jordan and Egypt. Conventional wisdom holds that civilization could only begin once people had stopped being nomadic, settled down and begun to live in farming communities. Only then, the argument goes, did people have the time and resources to create complex social systems and religious structures. It is now believed that this "revolution" was carried out by many hands, at many places, over thousands of years.

At the far northern edge of the Fertile Crescent sits Göbekli Tepe, meaning "Potbelly Hill" in Turkish. Its excavation has been a revelation. It suggests that the first sparks of civilization were driven by the need to worship. When the site was first discovered in the 1960s, it was dismissed as an abandoned medieval cemetery. The German archaeologist Klaus Schmidt decided to investigate the site again in 1994. So far only 1 acre (0.4 hectare) of a potential 22-acre (9-hectare) site has been excavated. Schmidt and his team mapped the entire summit using ground-penetrating radar and geomagnetic surveys, with the result that the site is thought to hold 16 other megalithic rings.

Göbekli Tepe is only one of the Fertile Crescent's many archaeological sites, testament to an extraordinarily rich and vivid human past. The sad truth is that in a politically volatile region, modern war is reshaping the archaeological landscape in new and unwelcome ways. Many historic cities, such as Nimrud and Nineveh, are now at risk of destruction. Much of the damage is premeditated and deliberate: the forces of so-called Islamic State actively seek to obliterate humanity's cultural treasures. Zealots used power tools to destroy the colossal lamassu, statues of terrifying human-headed winged beasts that stood guard at the Nergal Gate in Nineveh, and in Aleppo, Syria's oldest city, more than a hundred historic buildings have been damaged beyond repair.

DEVELOPMENT OF THE FERTILE CRESCENT

c.10,000 BCE
The earliest Neolithic places of worship are established at Göbekli Tepe

c.5500 BCE
Sumer is settled in Mesopotamia

2500 BCE–605 BCE
Assyrian empire

c. 2334 BCE–2154 BCE
Akkadian empire

1894 BCE
First Babylonian dynasty emerges, centring around Babylon

c.1600 BCE–c.1180 BCE
Hittite empire

c.1200 BCE–546 BCE
Lydian empire

911 BCE–609 BCE
Neo-Assyrian empire

626 BCE–539 BCE
Neo-Babylonian or Chaldean empire

678 BCE–549 BCE
Median empire

c.550 BCE–330 BCE
Achaemenid empire

330 BCE
Alexander the Great takes control of the Persian empire

READING THE HEAVENS

Klaus Schmidt and his team uncovered a series of mystical temples, in circles of beautifully carved pillars of stone. The temples' strange pillars are T-shaped, and the largest are 18 ft (5.5 m) high, weighing 17.5 tons (16 tonnes). Some are blank, but others are elaborately carved with imagery: writhing snakes, spiders, gazelles and bulls. Schmidt thought it possible that the pillars are stylized representations of human beings. Even more astonishing is that 6,000 years before the invention of writing, and seven millennia before the Great Pyramid of Giza was built, the central temple on the hill appears – to some – to map out the zodiac. It had long been thought that the first astronomers were the ancient Babylonians. Central to the temple known to the excavators as Temple D is a sequence of 12 pillars – the magical 12 that marks our calendar months today, the same 12 we use on our clocks. What is thought to be the world's oldest calendar (in monument form) was found in Scotland in 2004: it, too, works on a sequence of 12. The Warren Field site, however, dates from three and a half millennia later than Göbekli Tepe. Scientists from the University of Edinburgh believe that the first temple at Göbekli Tepe was a religious observatory, marking the history of comets and meteor showers. The bird and scorpion symbolism on one particular pillar, named the Vulture Stone, appears to document a comet strike around 11,000 BCE. If it happened at all, this devastating event would have caused environmental chaos and a mini ice age: whether or not it did occur is highly controversial among scientists. Carbon dating of charcoal deposits provides a date for the Vulture Stone that appears to mesh with new geological evidence from the Greenland ice core.

Cities of Beauty

From the Middle Ages, what most Europeans knew about ancient Mesopotamia was what they read in the Bible – stories of the Creation, the Flood and Babylon's Tower of Babel.

The gifted linguist Claudius James Rich became the Resident in Baghdad in 1808. Rich was the first antiquarian to examine the ancient site of Babylon, beginning in 1811–12. It was the starting point of Mesopotamian archaeology.

He gathered a huge collection of artefacts, but his main contribution was in the publication of his findings in a Viennese journal in 1812. There, he described the extraordinary Assyrian palace reliefs he had seen. He later travelled to Persepolis, Nimrud and Nineveh, documenting his journeys and the monuments he had encountered in a detailed memoir.

Home to the oldest library in the world, Nineveh was also excavated by Austen Henry Layard, who in 1842 found clay tablets there that gave the world the key to deciphering cuneiform. Layard also revealed the world's oldest story, the Epic of Gilgamesh.

With the assistance of his Iraqi student, Hormuzd Rassam, Layard uncovered two Assyrian palaces at Nimrud between 1845 and 1851: the Northwest Palace, built by King Ashurnasirpal II; and the Southwest Palace, built by King Esarhaddon. Layard believed he was excavating the Nineveh of the Bible. Later, he discovered that Nineveh in fact lay under the mound of Kouyunjik. When excavating the palace of King Sennacherib, he found thousands of objects, including many tablets, which took decades to decipher.

Following in Layard's footsteps was the German archaeologist, Robert Koldewey, who excavated at Babylon. Part of the new generation of systematic excavators who believed in documenting stratigraphy in detail, by 1917 he had made clear the rational city plan

A stone relief depicting the Assyrian king, Sargon II, with one of his dignitaries.

of Babylon, with its great north–south processional way, decorated in striking paving slabs of red and white. He also uncovered the Ishtar Gate of King Nebuchadnezzar which was later reconstructed in the Pergamon Museum in Berlin.

World War I briefly interrupted archaeological work in the Fertile Crescent, but it was resumed in the 1920s. Gertrude Bell was instrumental in founding the Iraq National Museum. While Leonard Woolley, who had worked with T. E. Lawrence during the war, led excavations at the Sumerian city of Ur in 1922–24.

With everything that was revealed by archaeologists in the area, a picture built up of just how much this amazing area had initiated: from the first agricultural systems and domestication of animals to the invention of irrigation and flood control and the pottery wheel, to the establishment of the first city states with recognizable social structures, organized religion and warfare.

The Richest City on Earth

Among the sites that have dazzled archaeologists during the last 200 years is the city of Persepolis, once the richest city on Earth. Set in the shadow of Iran's Mountains of Mercy, in its prime, Persepolis must have been truly other-worldly.

The grandson of Cyrus the Great, Darius I, established two new capitals during his time as ruler of the Achaemenid empire: the first at Susa, a thriving trade hub and his seat of government; and a second, largely ceremonial, city of unsurpassed grandeur at Persepolis.

Unfortunately, the city was sacked by Alexander the Great, supposedly in revenge for the destruction of Athens. Laid out on a remote, flat plain, Persepolis was one long hymn of triumph to Persian rule. A ceremonial stairway led up to a colossal gatehouse known as the Gateway of All Nations – not entirely a boastful description, given that by the time of Xerxes the Persians ruled 312 subject nations, each required to pay an annual tribute of gold.

The site was first excavated by Ernst Herzfeld from the American Oriental Institute in the 1930s, who uncovered the columns of a huge royal audience chamber known as the apadana, the Hall of a Hundred Columns; the Triplyon, where Xerxes received visiting dignitaries; the treasury and the harem.

Alphabet Men

How did the Phoenicians, once a flourishing civilization, vanish so completely?

The warlike seafarers occupied the Levant, the lush eastern Mediterranean coastline that is now divided between Lebanon,

Bas-relief carvings on the side of the ceremonial staircase at Persepolis.

Israel, Gaza and Syria between 1500 BCE and 539 BCE. They grew rich trading slaves, precious metals, wine, dye and pottery. They were so influential that their alphabet and language spread throughout the Mediterranean.

In 1923 the French archaeologist Pierre Montet discovered inscriptions made in the Phoenician alphabet on the sarcophagus of Ahiram, a king from the city of Byblos. There, Montet uncovered nine royal tombs in the city that gave its name both to books and to the Bible. In recent years, an excavation in the city of Sidon has revealed a fascinating collection of artefacts.

Despite their influence in the ancient world, most of the archaeological evidence for the great civilization comes from their neighbours. Reliefs found at the Assyrian city of Nineveh show Phoenician warships in great detail, including the dramatic eyes painted on their prows.

Phoenician explorers ventured as far afield as the Atlantic Ocean and established trading parternships with the British Isles and Scandinavia. They established colonies such as Carthage in North Africa, which they used to spread their culture, including the worship of Ba'al and other gods, around the Mediterranean.

UR – CITY OF THE MOON GOD

The city of Ur, named after the Moon god Urin, was occupied as early as the 7th millennium BCE. Early investigations in the 1920s led archaeologists to believe that they had found the site of the Biblical flood. However, the evidence of erosion was in fact due to regular smaller-scale flooding from the Euphrates and Tigris rivers.

One of the earliest Western visitors to Ur with archaeological ambitions was the Italian musician and author Pietro della Valle in 1625, who returned home with a number of inscribed bricks. The first significant excavation of the site was conducted by the British vice-consul at Basra, John George Taylor, in 1853–54, working on behalf of the British Museum. Taylor found a cylinder bearing the name of Nabonidus in the ziggurat that is now one of the major features of the site.

In 1923, during an expedition to Ur led by Leonard Woolley, excavations uncovered a royal cemetery whose oldest tombs dated as far back as 2600 BCE. From the tomb of Queen Puabi, who lived c.2500 BCE, emerged beautiful artefacts including a wooden harp, inlaid with exquisite ornamentation, and a bull's head, with staring lapis lazuli eyes. Nine superb headdresses were found, made from lapis and carnelian, their fringes of beech and willow leaves beaten from pure gold. This quality of workmanship is evidence of a stable, prosperous and technologically advanced society. Yet the headdresses lent a macabre glory to the skulls of the dead women wearing them.

Every single one of the 16 royal tombs was a place of ritual sacrifice. As many as 80 people at a time – courtiers, servants, soldiers and musicians – were sacrificed. Dressed in their most gorgeous finery, each held a cup of poison. Once the last had swallowed the lethal mix, the living lit ritual fires and celebrated the dead with a funeral banquet. We don't know if they volunteered or were forced.

In another tomb, Woolley discovered what is known as the Royal Standard of Ur, since he believed it would have been carried on a pole. The "war panel" shows the city's army marching to defeat a naked and quailing enemy. It is the earliest representation of a Sumerian military force.

Woolley's dig lasted until 1934. The objects uncovered were divided between the British Museum and the University of Pennsylvania Museum of Archaeology and Anthropology. The Iraqi authorities hope to develop the site as a tourist destination and, in 2009, agreed to work with the University of Pennsylvania on further excavations there.

LEONARD WOOLLEY (1880–1960)

Born in Clapton in east London, the son of a clergyman, Charles Leonard Woolley was interested in archaeology from an early age. Following his education at St John's School, Leatherhead and New College, Oxford, Woolley became an assistant director of Oxford's Ashmolean Museum in 1905. The following year, Arthur Evans suggested that Woolley should run excavations that were taking place at the Roman site of Corbridge, close to Hadrian's wall. It was the start of an archaeological career for which he later confessed that he was not really trained, having not studied archaeological methods, or knowing how to make a survey or a ground plan. In spite of his confessed lack of expertise, the Corbridge Lion, a magnificent sculpture of a lion attacking its prey dating from the 2nd or 3rd century CE, was found under his supervision.

In 1907, Woolley travelled to Nubia where he worked on the Eckley Coxe Expedition for the University of Pennsylvania Museum. For the next four years they surveyed and excavated sites including Areika, Buhen, and the Meroitic town of Karanog. Later, in 1912–14 he excavated the Hittite city of

Carchemish with T.E. Lawrence (see pages 61–2). When World War I broke out, Woolley was posted to Cairo (again with Lawrence). There he met the writer, administrator, and archaeologist Gertrude Bell. Moving to Alexandria, he was assigned to work on naval espionage. He was taken by the Turks when they captured a ship on which he was travelling and spent the next two years as a prisoner of war. At the end of the war he was awarded the Croix de Guerre by France.

At the start of 1922, Woolley led a joint expedition to Ur (now in south-east Iraq), on behalf of the British Museum and the University of Pennsylvania. His future wife Katherine was also on the expedition. Ur was the burial site of what may have been many Sumerian royals and the expedition made many spectacular discoveries (see page 122).

Woolley's assistant Max Mallowan was later married to Agatha Christie and her novel, *Murder in Mesopotamia*, was inspired by the discovery of the tombs.

By 1936, following the discoveries made at Ur, Woolley had become interested in finding ties between the civilizations of the ancient Aegean and of Mesopotamia. He was one of the first archaeologists to suggest that Noah's flood in the Book of Genesis was far more local than had previously been thought, identifying a flood-stratum at Ur: "… 400 miles long and 100 miles wide; but for the occupants of the valley that was the whole world".

During World War II Woolley joined the Monuments, Fine Arts and Archives Section of the Allied armies. At the end of the war he returned to Alalakh, where he continued to work from 1946 until 1949.

The Land of the Pharaohs

Ever since the discoveries of Napoléon's expedition, no other civilization has held such allure and excitement in the popular imagination as ancient Egypt. Archaeologists, historians and inquisitive travellers have flocked to the country to see its marvels for themselves.

The Egyptians had left so much to document their lives and tell their stories, but how to decipher their inscriptions, paintings and papyri?

In 1820, Jean-François Champollion began his race with the British polymath Thomas Young to decipher hieroglyphics. The key was a mysterious black stone, dug up by Napoléon's soldiers, and inscribed with three versions of a decree. Young had worked out the specific letters in Ptolemy V's name, found on the Rosetta stone and the Philae obelisk. Champollion was the first to realize that the language it showed was based on both pictures – ideographs – and phonetic sounds.

One beneficiary was Auguste Mariette. The Louvre Museum, keen to keep its lead in Egyptology, sent the young amateur devotee of hieroglyphics to buy new collections of papyri. Failing in this, he turned to a local Bedouin tribe, who took him to Saqqara. There, among a "spectacle of desolation" he found a huge temple complex, approached by a ceremonial avenue of sphinxes. When he returned to France, it was with a cache of some 2,500 statues, bronzes and cartouches. With the help of Isma'il Pasha, he made history in 1853 by opening a museum in Cairo. In 1858, he was appointed as director of the Department of Antiquities.

To Mariette's practical work on the ground would soon be added major advancements in techniques and scholarship with figures like William Flinders Petrie. Significant milestones in the history of archaeology, but Egyptology had further gifts to reveal.

One hundred years after Champollion had shown how to crack the code of hieroglyphs, another archaeologist, Howard Carter, took centre stage with a team of expert restorers, language experts, chemists and natural scientists. After various unsuccessful attempts, in November 1922, Carter was almost certain that he had found the tomb of the long lost "Boy King" Tutankhamun, in Luxor's Valley of the Kings.

The event generated more publicity than any other "moment" in the history of the science. Yet how much more extraordinary is it that the tomb of Ramesses II, "The Great", who died at the age of around 90, was just a few feet away?

In 1995, excavating underneath an area Carter had blocked with some debris, US archaeologist Kent Weeks discovered a hidden entrance, just 3½ ft (110 cm) wide. Inside, he expected to find a handful of chambers, but instead found himself in a vast labyrinth of underground hallways. Built by Ramesses II, who ruled Egypt from

Part lion, part human: the awe-inspiring Great Sphinx of Giza. The pyramids of Menkaure and Khafre lie in the background.

1279 BCE, the tomb (known as KV5) is utterly unique – the only royal "family tomb" in the Valley of the Kings.

Some researchers believe that Ramesses had more than 100 children: it's known for certain that he had 40 sons by his "primary" wives, as opposed to his concubines and slaves. Weeks and his fellow archaeologist, his wife Susan, have so far discovered 130 chambers at KV5.

Weeks is the director and founder of the magnificent Theban Mapping Project, which is working to improve – among many other things – the environmental conditions in tombs. Extremes of daily heat and nightly cold, combined with the moisture caused by the breath of thousands of tourists, are causing the exposed paint to peel off many tomb walls.

JEAN-FRANÇOIS CHAMPOLLION, THOMAS YOUNG AND THE DECIPHERING OF THE ROSETTA STONE

Jean-François Champollion's (1790–1832) skill with languages was apparent even as a young child; he gave his first public paper on the decipherment of the ancient Egyptian demotic script at the age of 16 and, even as a very young man he spoke fluent Coptic and Arabic and had been given a number of honorific posts in scientific circles. Napoleon's discoveries in Egypt during his campaign there from 1798 to 1801 led to a period of "Egyptomania" in France, and also brought into the spotlight the Rosetta Stone with its inscriptions in three languages. Subjects of fierce debate included the age of the Egyptian civilization, the purpose and development of hieroglyphic script, which language the script recorded, and to what extent the signs recorded the sound of speech (phonetic) or entire concepts (ideographic). Some believed that the script was used only for sacred and ritual functions, tied to esoteric and philosophical ideas, and did not record historical information. For these reasons they thought it might not be possible to decipher its meaning. Champollion's work was so significant because he showed that these assumptions were wrong, and enabled the retrieval of many kinds of information recorded by the ancient Egyptians.

Thomas Young (1773–1829) was another multi-talented individual. He joined the field of Egyptology in 1813, at a time when a number of other researchers already had significant work underway. He initially used the Egyptian alphabet of 29 letters built up by Johan David Åkerblad in 1802. By 1814, using a list with 86 demotic words, Young had translated the everyday text of the Rosetta Stone. He then moved on to the hieroglyphic alphabet but at first failed to realize that the demotic and hieroglyphic texts were in fact paraphrases and not straightforward translations. A number of Young's conclusions were published in an article on "Egypt" he wrote for the 1818 edition of the *Encyclopaedia Britannica*.

Young and Champollion did correspond and at first cooperated in their work, but from c.1815, tension arose between them and for many years they kept details of their work away from each other. In 1820, Champollion began his most serious attempt at the decipherment of hieroglyphic script and soon began to overshadow some of Young's most recent achievements.

By 1822, he had published his first breakthrough with the Rosetta hieroglyphs. He was able to show that the Egyptian writing system was in fact a combination of phonetic and ideographic signs – the first such script to be discovered. Young and many other scholars praised his work. In 1823 Young suggested in *Account of the Recent Discoveries in*

Hieroglyphic Literature and Egyptian Antiquities, that it would be only fair to have his own work recognized as the basis for Champollion's system. But although he had correctly discovered the sound value of six hieroglyphic signs, he had not discovered the grammar of the language. He did acknowledge that he was at a disadvantage because Champollion's knowledge of languages, such as Coptic, was much greater.

In his *Précis* of 1824 Champollion described how the hieroglyphic script could be deciphered, and showed the values of its phonetic and ideographic signs. Travelling to Egypt in 1829 he was able to read many hieroglyphic texts that had not been studied, and made many drawings of hieroglyphic inscriptions. Back home he was appointed professor of Egyptian history and archaeology at the Collège de France, but his poor health quickly forced him to give up teaching and he died in Paris of a stroke, aged just 41. His grammar of ancient Egyptian was published posthumously.

Champollion's decipherment led to a huge body of discussion and dissent among Egyptologists. He was criticized for having given insufficient credit to Young's early discoveries and suspected of plagiarism, while others disputed how accurate his decipherments were. Later findings and reaffirmation of his readings by scholars led to a wider acceptance of his work. Nearly 200 years later, although some argue that he should have more fully accepted the contributions of Young, Champollion's decipherment is now universally accepted, and has been the basis for all further developments in the field. He is regarded as the "Founder and Father of Egyptology".

A Matter of Life and Death

Each Pharaoh was seen as the progeny of the sun god who, with each reign, re-established order in a chaotic universe. Even now, Egyptian history is conventionally divided into the Old, Middle and New Kingdoms, divided by periods of supposed chaos.

Preserving the earthly body of god-kings like Ramesses II and Tutankhamun was essential: at stake was the continued wellbeing of Egypt. Once dead, the Pharaoh could communicate the needs of the people to the gods – so their mortuary shrines were intended to last. This, and the long series of spells known as *The Book of the Dead*, has given us a slightly distorted view, as if the ancient Egyptians spent their whole lives preparing for death.

Yet everyday Egypt was much more than morbid mummies and gloomy tombs. After two centuries of study, archaeologists are beginning to understand the culture more as a whole, and less as a sequence of Pharaohs and artefacts. We've even found examples of working class humour. In one illustration excavated from the artist's village of Deir el-Medina, a craftsman drew a cartoon mouse Pharaoh sitting in a chariot. He attacks a citadel of cats, a parody of the official art he had to produce by day in the Valley of the Kings.

In a painting on the east wall of the tomb of Paheri, in the wine region of El Kab, a woman is depicted demanding 18 cups of wine: "For I wish to drink until drunkenness; my inside is like straw." There were many ancient wine factories in Egypt. Wine had sacred power, signifying eternity because it gave new life to those who drank it... historians tell us that during the Festival of Bastet, even the cat god got drunk.

QUEEN NEFERTITI

Her name means "the beautiful one has come". Nefertiti was Akhenaten's favourite wife, famed for her beauty. The naturalism of this magnificent sculpture, made by the sculptor Thutmose c.1345 BCE, has made it a world-famous Egyptian icon. Yet it is uncharacteristic of most other Egyptian art. Thutmose's new creative freedom came from the artistic revolution that accompanied Akhenaten's extraordinary religious revolution. When the "Heretic

Pharaoh" decided to replace the traditional worship of many gods with a cult of a single god, the Aten, or sun disc, Nefertiti was at his side. They moved the entire Egyptian court to a new capital, Amarna. Three and a half thousand years later, the archaeologist Ludwig Borchardt found the bust during the first German excavation of the site. Borchardt hid the queen from Egyptian officials, and Nefertiti turned up in Berlin in 1925, causing a huge scandal.

Women's Work

Women had a far more equal role than the (mostly male) 19th-century archaeologists believed. Merneith, Khentkawes, Neithikret, Sobekneferu – there were many female rulers, including the famous Cleopatra of the later Ptolemaic dynasty, as well as influential consorts such as Queen Nefertiti, and we also know of two women viziers.

When female mummies with tattoos on their bodies were first discovered, most Egyptologists assumed they were women of low status, probably prostitutes or "dancing girls". Excavating ordinary village sites, William Flinders Petrie unearthed many sets of needles and dyes, indicating that commoners decorated their bodies. Yet the most famous of the tattooed female bodies was found in the tomb of a high-status official at Deir el-Bahari, normally an exclusively royal burial site.

Discovered in 1891 by the French Egyptologist Eugène Grébaut, Amunet was first thought to be a courtesan. She lived during Dynasty XI (c.2134–1991 BCE). Tattooed on the middle of her right thigh was a design of multiple diamond shapes; patterning her stomach are suggestively drawn circles, with undeniably carnal overtones. Amunet was a priestess of the sacred fertility goddess Hathor, and her story is part of the growing evidence that in ancient Egypt sexuality was intimately bound up with sacred ritual. It represented the link between the human and the divine: Nut, the sky goddess, was believed to swallow the sun each night and give birth to it the next morning.

More to Uncover

Nearly a century after Howard Carter, Egyptology is experiencing another Golden Age. Advances in sensing technology are driving this new wave of archaeology. In 2016, a 7,000-year-old "lost city" was unearthed near Sohag. In March 2017, part of a statue (possibly of Ramesses II) was discovered in the Matariya district of Cairo and in April, news came of the location of a new pyramid just north of Sneferu's bent pyramid in the Dahshur necropolis south of Cairo. The story of ancient Egypt continues....

THE GREATEST FIND IN HISTORY

"Can you see anything?" Lord Carnarvon asked, anxiously. Archaeologist Howard Carter was peering through a tiny hole, holding up a lighter. They had waited seven frustrating years for this moment. "Wonderful things," Howard Carter breathed.

A Team of Experts

Although Lady Evelyn Herbert, Lord Carnarvon's daughter, was the first to enter the tomb on that November day, the list of people involved in the opening of Tutankhamun's tomb reveals another truth: the sheer range of expertise Carter managed to enlist. There were 58 people present when he and Carnarvon first shone a light into Tutankhamun's resting place.

The multi-disciplinary team in this exemplary, scientifically planned project included philologist Sir Alan Gardiner, the Belgian archaeologist Jean Capart, the American archaeologist James Breasted, and John "Ora" Kinnaman, a Biblical scholar who would become the last remaining survivor of the Carter expedition, in 1961. The on-the-spot actions of chemist Alfred Lucas stabilized not just the grand chariots but the fragile linen gloves, wreaths of dried flowers, inscribed and painted boxes and chests crammed full of delicate fabrics, which would otherwise have fallen apart at a touch.

Cairo University's anatomist Douglas Derry analyzed Tutankhamun's mummy, realizing from the stage of fusion of the trochanter and femur bones that the king was only 19 years old, while Sir Archibald Douglas

Reid, an expert radiologist, X-rayed it, and Harry Burton photographed every find.

Unlike the tomb robbers who had gone before them, Carter's explorers were respectful, very conscious they were disturbing a pharaoh's grave. Inside the sepulchral chamber, they found a low door, which gave way to another small room. In the centre of the room stood a shrine-shaped chest of pure gold with a goddess at each of its four corners. Their arms stretched out from the darkness as if in pleading. There was such an emotional charge in their expressions that the whole party was moved: "I am not ashamed to confess," wrote Carter, "that the sight brought a lump to my throat."

The Tomb's Contents

Once Carter and his team had made their way down the stairs to Tutankhamun's tomb, they were faced with a corridor which led to an antechamber. There, they found what was described as "organized chaos", artefacts scattered all around due mostly to an unsuccessful attempt to rob the tomb.

The burial chamber, off which there were also a treasury room and an annexe, held four wooden shrines that surrounded Tutankhamun's sarcophagi. The king had three sarcophagi, placed one inside the other. The outermost was of rose granite and yellow quartzite, the middle showed a painted scene of the young pharaoh in ceremonial dress. The innermost sarcophagus was made of pure, polished gold inlaid with green feldspar, cornelian, and lapis lazuli. The wonderful final effigy took the form of a golden mask covering head and shoulders, its eyes set in aragonite and obsidian.

In total some 5,398 objects were catalogued by Carter and his team, and it took them ten years to do so. It was only in 2007 that Tutankhamun's mummy was finally returned to the tomb in the Valley of the Kings, where it is now on display.

The Curse of King Tut

The real story of the discovery of Tutankhamun's tomb is compelling enough, but add to that the so-called "curse", and you have true box office appeal. The pharaoh's protective symbol was the cobra. On the day Carter opened the tomb, a cobra got into the cage of his pet canary and killed it. After that, no fewer than 20 people connected with the opening of the tomb seem to have died in mysterious circumstances. They included Lady Carnarvon, who died of an infected mosquito bite four months later; the Louvre's representative, George Bénédite, who succumbed to heatstroke; the young Egyptian Prince Ali Kamel Fahmy Bey, who was shot by his French wife of six months; and Carter's secretary Richard Bethell, who was found dead in his club in Mayfair, the victim of a suspected smothering. These deaths and others gave rise to the story that has dogged Egyptian archaeology ever since.

Howard Carter (1874–1939)

Born in Kensington on 9 May 1874, Howard Carter spent much of his childhood with relatives in the Norfolk market town of Swaffham. There he visited Didlington Hall, home to the Amherst family and the repository of a substantial collection of Egyptian antiques. From then on Carter was enthused about the subject. At the age of just 17, he was sent by the Egypt Exploration Fund (EEF) to assist Percy Newberry in excavating and recording Middle Kingdom tombs at Beni Hasan. On that dig, Carter helped to improve the methods used for the copying of tomb decoration. The next year, he spent a season at Amarna, capital of the pharaoh Akhenaten, with Flinders Petrie. He worked from 1894 to 1899, with Édouard Naville at Deir el-Bahari, where he made copies of the wall reliefs in the temple of Hatshepsut.

In 1899 Carter was appointed chief inspector of the Egyptian Antiquities Service (EAS) and supervised excavations at Thebes (Luxor). In 1904, he moved to the Inspectorate of Lower Egypt where he developed systems for protecting and improving accessibility to existing excavation sites, and a grid-block system for searching for tombs. The Service also gave him funds to pursue his own excavation projects.

He resigned from the Antiquities Service in 1905 and in 1907 he was employed by Lord Carnarvon to supervise excavations of nobles' tombs in Deir el-Bahri, near Thebes. When, in 1914, Lord Carnarvon was given permission to dig in the Valley of the Kings, Carter was again employed to lead the work, shortly afterwards interrupted by the outbreak of World War I. He spent the war as a diplomatic courier and translator for the British government but was able to take up his excavations again in 1917.

By 1922, Lord Carnarvon had become dissatisfied with the lack of results and told Carter that he would fund him for one more season

to make a significant find in the Valley of the Kings. Returning to the Valley, he looked again at a line of huts abandoned a few seasons earlier. On 4 November a young water boy fell over a stone. It was the top of a flight of steps cut into the bedrock. Carter had the steps dug out until the top of a mud-plastered doorway stamped with cartouches appeared. Ordering the staircase to be re-covered, Carter sent a telegram to Carnarvon, who arrived on 23 November.

On 26 November 1922, Carter made a small breach in the doorway to see the treasures inside (see pages 135–6). He spent the next ten years cataloguing the "wonderful things" they had found within.

Although he had been instrumental in one of the greatest archaeological finds of all time, Howard Carter was not rewarded by the British government, although he did receive the Order of the Nile, third class, from King Fuad I of Egypt. Once the tomb had been cleared and catalogued, he retired from archaeology. He became an agent acting on behalf of collectors and museums. His 1924 lecture tour of Britain, France, Spain and especially the US, led to a great surge of interest in Egyptology. He died in London on 2 March 1939, aged 64.

The Mystery of the Indus

The urban-based civilization that arose along the banks of the Indus River, running across what today is northwest India and Pakistan, was the third to develop in the ancient world. It would become the largest of all, at its peak extending over 600,000 miles^2 (1 million km^2). Emerging from about 2800 BCE, and fully formed from about 2500 BCE, at its peak the civilization comprised as many as 100 towns, as well as many substantial cities including Dholavira, Lothal, and the civilization's two largest and most dominant, Mohenjo-Daro and Harappa. And yet, for all its sweep, the Indus Valley culture suddenly began to decline around 1900 BCE.

It was made possible by the 1,800-mile (3,000-km)-long Indus river and its tributaries, which run across the otherwise arid wastes of a vast plain between Baluchistan, mountainous and hostile, to the west, and the Thar Desert to the east. From here, the Indus flows into the Arabian Sea. Like the Nile, the Indus floods every spring, though in the case of the Indus it occurs as a result of melting Himalayan snow. The resulting irrigation and rich alluvial silts these floods provided created a narrow but fertile strip that naturally lent itself to settlement, giving rise to an astonishingly successful society, known as the Indus Valley Civilization or Harappan. Its development paralleled those of Mesopotamia, Egypt and China, producing a society that was literate, organized and, above all, urban.

Agriculture was nonetheless its bedrock. Wheat and barley, sown in the spring and requiring minimal attention, were the chief crops, though peas, too, were grown, and in some areas, especially further east, rice. Cotton is known to have been cultivated and woven for clothes. Among those animals most successfully domesticated were cattle, sheep, goats, boars and elephants. Whether as a food source or as beasts of burden, camels, too, were essential in the success of this new world.

Discovering a New Civilization

Not the least remarkable aspect of the Indus Valley cities is the fact that, in striking contrast to the first cities of Mesopotamia, China and Egypt, until the 19th century it was a world whose existence was entirely unknown. It wasn't until the 1830s that a British adventurer and one-time soldier, Charles Masson, discovered Harappa, the first of many Indus Valley sites. Masson had little idea of its significance, and it was only after 1924 that the first excavations of the Indus Valley sites began at Mohenjo-Daro, discovered in 1920 by the leading Indian archaeologist of the time, R. D. Banerji.

A team from the Archaeological Survey of India led by K. N. Dikshit undertook these first investigations. Further work was carried out under a team led by British archaeologist John Marshall in 1925. Work on the site continued in the 1930s, conducted by the most noted archaeologist of the period, the flamboyant Mortimer Wheeler, director of the Indian Archaeological Survey between 1944 and 1948. Excavation resumed in 1945, reaching a peak in the mid-1960s with a team lead by an American archaeologist, George Dales. Further work was then suspended as anxieties grew about damage caused by the weathering of the structures exposed by the digs. In 2015, however, work was resumed under the aegis of Pakistan's National Fund for Mohenjo-Daro, which used the less damaging technique of dry core drilling. First results suggested that the site was very much larger than initially believed, even if its exact size remains a matter of speculation today.

CHARLES MASSON (1800–1853)

James Lewis, a British East India Company soldier and explorer – and sometime intelligence agent – used the pseudonym, Charles Masson. He was the first European to see the ruins of Harappa near Sahiwal in Punjab, now in Pakistan.

Born in London, Masson joined the Bengal Artillery wing of the East India Company Army in India, serving at the Battle of Bharatpur. In 1827, while based at Agra, he deserted and, accompanied by a colleague, travelled through parts of British-controlled Punjab. When they reached Ahmadpur, they were taken on by Josiah Harlan as mounted orderlies in his expedition to overthrow the regime in Kabul, Afghanistan. Shortly afterwards, near Dera Ghazi Khan, Masson deserted once again.

He was re-employed by the British East India Company, Bombay Government between 1833 and 1838, during which time he excavated over 50 Buddhist sites around Kabul and Jalalabad in south-eastern Afghanistan.

He also put together a large collection of small objects and many coins, mainly from the site at Bagram (the ancient Alexandria on the Caucasus), north of Kabul. From 1827–42, it is estimated that he collected around 47,000 coins and his final collection totalled 60,000.

Masson wrote of his exploration of the ruins of Harappa, in his illustrated book *Narrative of Various Journeys in Balochistan, Afghanistan and The Panjab*. He also visited the North-West Frontier Province and Balochistan, serving as an agent of the East India Company. It seems that he left his mark elsewhere in the region in the 1930s a French archaeological party found an inscription in the caves above one of the Bamiyan Buddhas (now sadly destroyed) that read:

> *If any fool this high samootch explore,*
> *Know Charles Masson has been here before.*

An Unknown Society

For all of the excavation work, the Indus Valley's systems of government, religion and social organization today remain tantalizingly little known. No one can say if there were kings, nor even if a kind of single proto-state existed. The role of religious leaders, if any, remains equally elusive.

The simple reason for this is that no single substantial written record has come to light. Even so, this was a literate civilization: more than 3,500 individual inscriptions have been found on pottery, on clay seals, on bronze vessels and on fragments of ivory. At least 400 different symbols have been identified. Without a more substantial manuscript, the so-called Indus Valley Script remains undeciphered.

Experts believe the language may belong to the Dravidian group and is a very distant ancestor of today's Tamil and Malayalam.

Despite the absence of any written record, the archaeological record, while incomplete, has revealed a well-ordered society of exceptional sophistication and reach. At its peak, the 99 acres (40 hectares) Mohenjo-Daro site is estimated to have had a population of 40,000. The city was laid out on a regular grid pattern, its main street never less than 30 ft (9 m) wide. A central citadel is thought to have been a religious, ceremonial and administrative hub.

One of Mohenjo-Daro's most startling features is the 40 ft (12m) long, 13 ft (7m) wide and 11 ft (3 m) deep "Great Bath". Its purpose may have been purely sanitary – the city boasted 80 public lavatories as well as a complex system of sewers and drains: similarly, every house had its own well. But it may also have had a ritual function as a place of purification, with water as the great cleanser and healer. In much the same way, it has been suggested that the adjoining "College Building" was home to a priestly caste.

A series of residential districts spread out from this central core. In some, the airy, flat-roofed houses were large and built around courtyards. Most inhabitants, though, lived in single-room dwellings, a series almost of tenements. The fact that in almost every Harappan settlement except Dholavira, the bricks used are of exactly the same size: 9 in x 5 in x 3 in (23 cm x 13 cm x 8 cm) is a further indicator of centralized social organization. A series of granaries provided storage for the region's agricultural products. As in the case of many other ancient civilizations, most of the clay seals so far discovered in the Indus Valley record financial transactions.

One of the earliest mysteries of the Indus Valley civilization was the discovery of a series of sites found to the east of the Indus river in a region that today is unremittingly hostile desert. How could these sites have been established with no ready access to water? The answer, simply, is that there once was water, supplied by a river, the Ghaggar, similarly fed by melting Himalayan snows, whose course may have been catastrophically diverted by what is presumed to have been an earthquake. All that remains above ground today is a series of unpromising salty and stagnant pools. In fact, the river still flows underground; its surprise rediscovery in 1990 has transformed the region.

Built along the Sabarmati River on the Gulf of Khambhat, Lothal was discovered in 1954. Excavated by the Archaeological Survey of India between 1955 and 1960, the city was a gateway to the Indus civilization. Artefacts show it was a key link in the maritime trade routes that connected the Indus Valley with the wider world. It houses the oldest purpose-built dock yet found. The impressive dock also boasted a lock with wooden gates, designed to counter and exploit the substantial tidal range of the Gulf of Khambhat, allowing access at all times.

An example of a stamp seal from the Indus Valley. Stamp seals were used to mark an item to show ownership and as a display of status.

An Industrial Indus

Able to barter a stable food supply for raw materials, above all copper and bronze, a series of thriving proto-industries developed in the region. Along with essentials such as pottery, a wide range of goods was produced: weapons, mirrors, jewellery, ceramics and even razors. These were traded to Persia and Afghanistan, hauled overland by bullock carts, then the primary means of transport in the region.

Indus Valley sailors also pioneered maritime routes, taking advantage of the monsoon winds of the region. In 2300 BCE, Sargon, the ruler of Agade in Mesopotamia, recorded the arrival of ships from the Indus Valley. By the end of the 3rd millennium BCE, the Indus Valley was at the centre of a great trading network that straddled the Indian Ocean, central Asia and what would later be known as the Silk Road.

The steady accumulation of the archaeological evidence suggests that the Indus Valley was among the most dynamic civilizations of the ancient world. Its influence on the later development of India is plain. It is possible, too, that the origins of Hinduism, the world's oldest religion, lie here: Hindu means "of the Indus".

No very compelling reasons have been offered to explain why the Indus Valley civilization ended so abruptly. It may have been the result of a change in the course of the Indus river itself, which rendered once fertile regions barren. Climate change has also been suggested. All that can be said with certainty is that a vigorous and thriving society was brought to a more or less sudden end.

Yet its enduring significance cannot be overstated: the world that was never less than uncertain, the Indus Valley was the site of one of the first civilizations that transformed the way we live, replacing the hunter-gatherer lifestyle with settled agricultural and industrial societies. Farming based on the Indus River permitted the development of new, urban-based ways of life which in turn allowed the development of élites.

Much as the collapse of the society of the Mediterranean and the Levant towards the end of the 2nd millennium BCE was followed by a kind of dark age about which little can be said, the collapse of the Indus Valley civilization between 1900 and 1700 BCE was followed by a long gap in the archaeological and historical record.

It may have been filled c.1500 BCE by the arrival of Aryan peoples migrating from the northwest, although again, there is no indisputable evidence of this. Wherever they came from and however much they may have exploited and learned from what remained of the Harappan world, they would be the next vital influence on the development of India.

THE CITY OF STONE

Thanks to its immense stone-built reservoirs, Dholavira is perhaps the most impressive Indus Valley site of all. The city was only discovered in 1968 and first excavated in 1989 by a team from the Archaeological Survey of India led by R. S. Bisht. Given the paucity of information about the Indus Valley cities, the results of the dig have added enormously to our knowledge of the period, and suggest that so large and precisely built a city could only have been the result of concerted central direction. The objects discovered include pottery, bronze, jewellery, terracotta statuary, a series of seals and, at ten characters in length, the longest continuous segment of the Indus script ever found.

Dholavira presents an even more compelling case for the sophistication of the Indus Valley. Whereas both Mohenjo-Daro and Harappa were built almost exclusively of baked bricks, Dholavira was built of stone. This reflects both the availability of stone as a building material and highlights a remarkable degree of centralized organization and technical capability.

The city's most impressive features are its 16 stone-built reservoirs, the largest 260 ft (79 m) long and 23 ft (7 m) deep. These indicate that the Indus Valley civilization's management of water was exceptional.

In a region where several years might pass without rain, Dholavira created a vast system, using dams and reservoirs to assiduously collect and store both the river and rainwater that was vital to its prosperity.

At the heart of Dholavira there was a well, 13 ft (4 m) across and 65 ft (20 m) deep, lined with precisely engineered masonry. Its importance was plainly more than merely practical: it made very clear that water was, as has been said, "the mother of civilization".

The Valley of the Huang He River

Uniquely among the world's great civilizations, China can claim an unbroken line of descent from its first major civilization, the Shang, to the present. Culturally, linguistically, economically and politically, Shang China established a common Chinese identity that has endured for close to 4,000 years, despite periodic, convulsive and hugely destructive crises, natural and man-made. It represents an astonishing continuity. With the emergence of Shang China, by about 1800 BCE, China laid claims to levels of technical sophistication and social organization unmatched by Western civilizations for centuries.

As with the other civilizations of the ancient world, it was a river valley, in this case the Yellow River watercourse in north-central China, that made this transformation possible. It built on a much earlier agricultural transformation, as hunter-gatherers gradually developed settled agriculture, based on millet in the north of the country and based on rice in the south. Similarly, animals were domesticated, pigs and sheep in particular. Yet despite the development of a written script from about 1400 BCE, one that remains the basis of written Chinese today, the archaeological record has still proved critical in understanding how China under the Shang and later dynasties was formed. It has revealed a society of exceptional sophistication, which was disposing of no less exceptional resources.

China was first settled by early hominids perhaps 500,000 years ago. *Homo sapiens* seems to have become established there as early as 30,000 years ago. A cave dwelling in Jiangxi Province, the Xianren Cave, excavated in the 1990s, has produced evidence not just of early rice cultivation but of the earliest pottery ever found, dating from around 20,000 years ago.

THE CRAFTS OF PAN-P'O-TS'UN

A Neolithic village at Pan-p'o-ts'un (Banpo) in Shensi (Shaanxi), dating from between 5000 and 3000 BCE and excavated in the 1950s, has revealed a substantial village, clay-walled with thatched houses clustered around a central hall 44 ft (13.5 m) long. Pottery kilns and workshops were found along with a variety of stone and bone tools. By about 3000 BCE, there is evidence of towns rather than villages. More advanced craftsmanship was developed as well as a clear taste for luxury goods, carved jade above all, valued by the Chinese even more highly than gold.

Societal Development

The transition from these early societies to the vastly more sophisticated, urban-based world of the Shang was never clear-cut. But when it came, the emergence of a literate, highly stratified, technically accomplished warrior civilization was astonishing. It marked, too, the birth of the Bronze Age in China, a point highlighted by the increasing production of bronze-cast objects, many exceptionally intricate and elaborate.

The political complexion of Shang China is uncertain. Was it a centralized state ruling over much of northern China from its various capitals, six in all, along the Yellow River valley? Or was it, as seems more probable, a more loosely organized confederation of essentially clan-based domains? The best evidence for it comes from two sources: oracle bones and those Shang tombs that have been excavated.

A bronze ritual set from the Zhou dynasty.

Together, they highlight another fundamental fact of Shang China: that religion, which mostly took the form of ancestor worship, a cult deemed worthy only of the aristocracy, seems to have been a private matter. There can be little doubt that a priestly élite existed: oracle bone divination would have been impossible without it. Yet the kind of substantial temples found in Mesopotamia and Egypt seem not to have existed.

ORACLE BONES

Shang oracle bones were first found in 1899 in the most important Shang archaeological site yet discovered, Yinxu, today in the modern city of Anyang. Their significance was first realized by the director of the Imperial College, Wang Yirong. By 1917, they had been deciphered by another Chinese scholar, Wang Guowei. It was he who realized that their script, part phonetic, part pictographic, was essentially unchanged in modern Chinese. Oracle bones were generally the shoulder bones of a beast of burden, typically water buffalo or cattle, that were heated until they cracked. The resulting cracks were then interpreted or divined by a seer, the result recorded in writing on the bone itself. Such divinations could cover almost any subject, from the weather to major military campaigns. However brief their texts, they are an essential window into the world of Shang China.

The Grave of Fu Hao

The Shang tombs have made very clear not just the importance of religion in Shang China but the astonishing riches that were lavished on it. The most important of these tombs are in Yinxu. Even if what is presumed to have been their exceptionally rich contents were mostly subsequently looted, what remains makes vividly clear the reach and potency of Shang China. In 1976, an unlooted tomb was found. It is the grave of Fu Hao, one of the wives of the Shang king Wu Ding, thought to have died in about 1200 BCE. If hardly on the startling scale of the 3rd century BCE tomb of the great Qin emperor Shi Huangdi and his Terracotta Army of 6,000 soldiers, it nonetheless contained 755 jade objects, 564 bone objects (500 hairpins among them), 468 bronze objects, 63 stone objects, 11 pieces of pottery, 5 ivory objects and 6,900 cowrie shells, then used as a form of currency. Also found were the skeletons of six dogs and 16 ritually sacrificed humans. This indicated a highly stratified society.

By about 1030 BCE, Shang rule had been overthrown, replaced by the Zhou, an ethnic group from northwest China. The Zhou dynasty presents an obvious paradox. In the first place, the centralized authority of the Shang was abandoned in favour of a series of domains, almost like European fiefdoms, awarded to those loyal to the Zhou. But in 771, the majority of these feudal territories broke away from the Zhou, becoming in effect independent during the Spring and Autumn period. Almost 100 such rival states appeared. The Zhou, with their power greatly reduced, became merely one among them. It was a process accompanied by almost constant warfare. The years between 472 and 221 BCE, when these numerous petty states were reduced to 20, as conquest on a startling scale occurred, were aptly named the Warring States period.

But whatever its political fragmentation, whatever the consequences of centuries of brutal warfare, China itself, in the sense of an area that became recognizably Chinese culturally, was enormously extended. By the 5th century BCE the Yangtze valley to the south and much of Manchuria to the north had been definitively integrated into this Chinese cultural world. At the same time, significant technological advances were made and many Chinese political institutions reformed and strengthened. By the 4th century BCE, the leading Chinese states commanded armies whose combined numbers approached one million. Some battles saw in excess of 100,000 men deployed. Warfare on this scale was unknown in any other part of the world. In Europe it wouldn't be matched until the 16th century.

A New Level of Craftsmanship

At the same time, levels of craftsmanship reached new heights. As early as the 11th century BCE, at the start of the Zhou dynasty, bronze workers were capable of works as refined as the Kang Hou gui or urn, a ritual food vessel. (The urn is important, too, as evidence of Zhou feudal grants of territory: an inscription around its lip records that territories in Wey were granted to Kang Hou, the Marquis of Kang, brother of King Wu, for his suppression of a Shang rebellion.)

From c.650 BCE, iron began to be used for the first time. From the 5th century BCE, as stone and bone tools were increasingly replaced by iron implements, agricultural production was hugely boosted. The introduction of coins, widely circulated by the 4th century BCE, was similar evidence of growing economic sophistication.

The technological prowess of China in this otherwise tumultuous period is very well illustrated by the Tonglushan mine, discovered in Hubei province in 1973 and excavated over the following 12 years.

The excavations revealed a site that was genuinely a kind of proto-industrial complex, in continuous use for 1,000 years from about 700 BCE. Several hundred mining shafts, originally lined by bamboo, were discovered along with a series of smelting furnaces and around 1,000 mining tools. Evidence for sophisticated ventilation systems was found. Methods for removing ground-water also came to light during excavation. The complex covered an area of some 20 acres (9 hectares). It is estimated that 80,000 tons of copper was produced here, all of it by hand.

It was exactly this kind of technological and organizational superiority, combined with an ever-stronger sense of a unified

The Tonglushan mine was an ancient industrial complex consisting of hundreds of mining shafts and furnaces.

Chinese identity, that would make China so formidable a force when, in 221 BCE, it was forcibly re-united under the single rule of the Qin emperor Shi Huangdi.

Classical & Early
Civilizations
in Europe

Classical Greece

High society was obsessed with the virtues of classical Greece. In the 18th century, aristocrats from across Europe flocked to Greece as part of the "Grand Tour". At the same time, academia began to argue about the nature of its democracy and philosophy.

Finding the site of Olympia, ancient Greece's most important religious, sporting and political centre, was a sort of Holy Grail for European antiquarians. The ancient Greeks had celebrated their great athletes by commissioning bronze and marble statues, and the experts believed they would find "wonderworks by the thousand" if they could discover the site where the ancient Olympics were held.

By 1723, antiquarians such as the French scholar Bernard de Montfaucon had spent many years trying to identify the site. In fact, most of Olympia's largest statuary had already been looted in antiquity by the Romans, including the famed gold and ivory statue of Zeus, the king of the gods, carved by the great sculptor Phidias.

In 1766, the British Society of Dilettanti commissioned a young architect called Richard Chandler to try and find it. After three long years of wandering, he discovered some likely looking ruins in the wild mountains of the Peloponnese, hidden in an overgrown vineyard. It wasn't until 1829, however, that the French excavated the site, uncovering the Temple of Zeus. As was by now traditional, they shipped the finest pieces of sculpture back to the Louvre. This prompted a fiery correspondence with Greeks inspired by the ideals of the French revolution. Why shouldn't those ideals of freedom, of ownership by the people, for the people, apply to them?

The Greek Archaeological Service was set up in 1833, immediately after Greece established its independence from the Ottoman Empire, under the control of the Ministry of Culture. However, the feverish interest from western European countries was such that many institutions were established throughout the middle and latter part of the 19th century, with the French School at Athens being the first in 1846.

Eventually, it was the Germans who were given exclusive rights to excavate Olympia, under a team led by Friedrich Adler, Richard Bohn and Ernst Curtius. They were assisted by Wilhelm Dörpfeld, whose work at Mycenae and with Heinrich Schliemann on the site of Troy would make him one of the leading archaeologists of Bronze Age sites. He later revealed the Hekatompedon temple at the Acropolis in Athens.

Greece became an inspiration for academics, artists and writers alike: the poet Byron set off for Messolonghi, a hub of the Greek War of Independence, where he died of a fever in 1824. Every night, the future Ludwig I of Bavaria read aloud from his original Greek version of the Gospels, a bust of Homer by his side. The philosopher Wilhelm Traugott Krug tried to establish "Philhellene" societies, supporting volunteers who would travel in the Greek – and Christian – cause. The three great German poets Goethe, Schiller and Hölderlin might have lived and breathed in Germany, but the mainstay of their poetic imaginations was Greece.

Schliemann's work at Troy and Mycenae fuelled the public's interest. His discovery of "Priam's Treasure" and the so-called "Mask of Agamemnon" were extremely newsworthy.

Around the same time as Dörpfeld and Schliemann were at work, so the new Keeper of the Ashmolean Museum in Oxford, Arthur Evans, began to plan one of the greatest excavations ever to take place in Greece, on the island of Crete.

A devoted scholar, Evans was the complete antithesis of Schliemann. Still, he had keenly followed the debate about whether Homer's "Troy" could really be a genuine city, as opposed to the figment of a poetic mind. Evans had even visited Schliemann on site. Like Schliemann, he was a wealthy man. Once he heard tales of exquisite antiquities being dug up on the island, there was no holding him back. By chance, Evans had got hold of some strange golden seal-stones in an Athens flea market. Amulet-sized and beautifully engraved, they were decorated with an unknown, pictographic script. He had a hunch that the strange writing was evidence of an entire lost civilization waiting to be discovered.

The fact that Crete was embroiled in a war did not stop him. As a result of his journalistic support for the island's fledgling republic, Evans secured the sole rights of excavation at the place he had set his sights on: the Kafala Hill. After Crete had won its independence, Evans used an inheritance to purchase the site in 1900. What he discovered there would be a sensation.

Evans devoted his life to Knossos, though he also played a key part in the development of the Ashmolean and the British Museum.

THE MASK OF AGAMEMNON

This is a funeral mask made for a king of kings. It's also one of the most powerful and compelling archaeological discoveries of all time. The thin, haughty face, portrayed in beaten gold with astonishing naturalism, is on display in the National Archaeological Museum of Athens. The man who supposedly lay in death beneath this golden mask is one of the strongest but darkest characters in ancient Greek literature. Impatient and quick to anger, Agamemnon was the quarrelsome, stubborn and arrogant leader of the Achaeans, who massed against Troy. So that he could win in battle, he sacrificed his own daughter. When he returned from war triumphant, his wife murdered him. The only problem is that this is not Agamemnon. The shaft graves where this treasure was found date from 1600 BCE, 300 years before Homer's account of the Trojan War.

The Ravages of War

You don't need to be a specialist to know how much damage can be done to a precious site by an invading or occupying army: the deliberate and systematic destruction of the Warsaw ghetto by the Nazis in World War II is one horrific example. The nearest miss in archaeological history, though, has to be the almost total destruction of the Parthenon during the Great Turkish War of 1683–89.

Even in its ruined state today, the temple remains a symbol of civilization, a hymn to the extraordinary aesthetic and cultural accomplishments of ancient Greece. Yet it nearly wasn't so.

Possibly believing that the Venetian commander Morosini would not attack a building of such importance, the occupying Turkish soldiers fortified the Parthenon and used it to store their gunpowder. They were sorely mistaken. On 26 September 1685, a Venetian mortar round scored a direct hit, and blew up the gunpowder store. The titanic explosion came very close to razing the greatest example of classical Greek architecture ever built. The occupying troops took to grinding up slabs of fallen marble to make yet more gunpowder.

For the next 150 years, the building endured further sporadic looting, until, in 1801, the Earl of Elgin bought some of the remaining sculptures and friezes, and had them shipped to London.

Arguments about whether or not the friezes should be returned to the Greeks continue to rage, but at least they are now being expertly preserved. Other world-class archaeological sites have not been so lucky.

A King's Legacy

Now in modern-day Turkey, Ephesus was initially founded by Ionian Greek colonists in the 10th century BCE. Under the rule of the Lydian kings it became one of the wealthiest cities in the world, a centre of learning and a place where women enjoyed rights and privileges equal to men; there are records of female artists, sculptors and teachers.

The city became famous for the vast Temple of Artemis, which was completed c.550 BCE, and its Roman creations, the Library of Celsus and a 25,000-seat amphitheatre. This marvel in white marble became one of the seven wonders of the ancient world. After flourishing under the Roman Republic, much of Ephesus, like Rome itself, was destroyed by the Goths in 263 CE. What's left remains so spectacular that tourists flock to the ruined city every year.

In recent years, an international team of archaeologists began excavating the huge, wealthy 1st–2nd century CE residential district whose ruins lie adjacent to the Library of Celsus. The entire 43,000 ft² (4,000 m²) site has been covered by a clever roofing membrane, which allows in 90 per cent of the light but keeps out much of the heat. The archaeologists needed all the comfort – and help – they can get. They faced a monumental task: one team restoring a single marble panel had to reassemble 120,000 small fragments – and most of the fragments were the same colour. Political concerns ended the project prematurely in 2016 after a diplomatic row between Austria and Turkey.

Alexander the Great liberated Ephesus from the Persians in 334 CE. On his way to founding what would then become the world's largest empire, which stretched across three continents and covered some 2,000,000 miles² (5,200,000 km²), Alexander offered to rebuild the Temple of Artemis, which had been burned down by a madman. Alexander felt some connection with it: it had been destroyed on the night of his birth.

Alexander's sudden death, in Babylon at the age of only 33, is truly perplexing. It remains one of the longest-running mysteries of all time. The military leader was so strong, so capable, that even his own troops considered him almost a god. Was it malaria? Poisoning? Accounts say that there was no vomiting. Perplexingly, the body failed to show any signs of decay for six days, despite the intense heat. It was always presumed that he was buried in Egypt, and without significant remains, it has been impossible for archaeology to help resolve the debate. Then, in 2012, a phenomenally large tomb was uncovered on the Kasta Hill at Amphipolis, in northern Greece, a site close to the Aegean port that Alexander used for his fleet. The tomb is enormous, its massive perimeter wall, clad in dressed marble from the island of Thassos, is 1,630 ft (497 m) long. Excavations of the entire site will take many years.

Clearly, someone very important was buried here. Excitement mounted as evidence of a huge monument emerged. Topped with a statue of a lion, it would have been clearly visible from sea. So far, only two years of excavation have been funded. Excavators are attempting to stabilize the tomb contents, rescuing the paintings from the ravages of humidity.

Is this Alexander's tomb? Or was it built for Hephaestion, Alexander's childhood friend and lover? Like Alexander, Hephaestion died suddenly, succumbing to an unidentified ailment in 324 BCE, at Ecbatana in Iran.

The lead archaeologist at Amphipolis, Katerina Peristeri, is convinced that the site began as a funerary monument for Hephaestion: there is an inscription on one wall that suggests that Alexander himself commissioned it, and had it built between 325 and 300 BCE. There, though, the certainties end. Owing to the work of looters, the stratigraphy has been destroyed, and most of the grave goods have gone. Accelerator mass spectrometry, (AMS) analysis may tell us more about the bones, but the project as a whole will take years to complete.

THE LIBRARY OF CELSUS

The original library was constructed c. AD 114–17 in honour of the Roman Senator Tiberius Julius Celsus Polemanaenus, a wealthy citizen of Ephesus, who was buried in a sarcophagus beneath the library, which was in fact built as his mausoleum. The library was reputedly the third largest of the ancient world and supposedly housed approximately 12,00 scrolls. The façade was re-erected between 1970 and 1978.

THE ERECTHEUM "CARYATIDS"

The six "caryatids" maidens of the Erectheum in Athens support the heavy entablature, a metaphor in marble. Carya, a city in the Peleponnese, had decided to support the Persians. After their victory, the Athenians pursued its inhabitants mercilessly, killing all the menfolk, selling the women into slavery, and then immortalizing their suffering on the Acropolis.

A Never-ending Story

Greece has such a rich history that it is difficult to imagine more fertile ground for archaeology. A team from the University of Cincinnati uncovered the grave of a man, now known as the Griffin Warrior, at the Palace of Nestor at Pylos. The remains of this Mycenaean grandee were surrounded and covered by bronze, silver and gold objects, shedding light on his status and the funerary procedures of males of the period.

As recently as 2016, the remains of a 2,500-year-old city near the village of Vlochós, about five hours north of Athens, were discovered by a team of Swedish archaeologists from the University of Gothenburg.

The Legend of the Minotaur

"Out in the middle of the wine-dark sea there is an island called Crete, a rich and lovely land, washed by the sea on every side... Among the ninety cities is Knossos, a great city; and there Minos was nine years king, the boon companion of mighty Zeus."

The *Odyssey* (Book 19) Homer

The *Iliad* and its counterpart the *Odyssey*, with their tales of epic heroism and impossibly beautiful women, were founding texts of Western civilization. Embedded in these Greek myths was an enticing idea: that once there had been a lost island, the true home of the gods of myth. Terrifying tales emerged from the island's mists: of Icarus, who flew too close to the sun; Theseus, who killed the grisly half-bull, half-man monster called the Minotaur, and the great king Minos who had fathered the monster, and kept him lurking in his labyrinth. According to myth, Zeus himself was born on Crete.

Evans's dig at Knossos began in March 1900. One day, one of the local workmen suddenly cried out in fear. He had found a "black devil" he shouted, shying away from the sinister head he had plucked out from the soil. A black, red-eyed bust of a bull's head, with huge, gilded curved horns and a rippled neck was staring back at him. Made out of precious stone and mother of pearl, the "rhyton" found that day is more than 3,500 years old.

The drama convinced Evans that he had found the true home of the mythical King Minos. More artefacts and fragments of frescoes told him that the people who had lived at Knossos worshipped the bull. The labyrinth of buildings emerging from the ground was truly ancient, older by far than Athens' magnificent Parthenon, built c.450 BCE when classical Greece was at its height.

Evans had unearthed an entire, lost civilization, documented by many beautiful works of art. Frescoes depicted a sophisticated culture based on colour, dance, swimming, music, acrobatic bull-jumping and joy. The first level excavated dates from c.1900 BCE, but was built on the ruins of a settlement that was even older. Knossos was as ancient as the oldest Egyptian pyramids: contemporary with the time of the Egyptian Old Kingdom, 2575–2134 BCE.

The bull's-head rhyton found at Knossos.

The Bronze Age "palace" was monumental in size and scale, built using fine ashlar masonry. It held many shrines, and a Throne Room, with a red panel at the centre of the floor: a colour known to be associated with the underworld.

In what Evans called the "Hall of the Double Axes", a private chamber with an inner space closed off by 11 sets of double doors, he found the dissolved remains of what most experts have agreed was a throne. It rested not upon a stone dais, but on four fluted wooden columns.

As find after find built up, including many tablets inscribed with an early form of writing, he realized that the lives of the inhabitants had been luxurious. The palace had running water, baths and even alabaster windows. Both women and men wore exotic jewellery and make up. Men wore ceremonial headdresses and flared kilts; for ceremonies, the women went bare-breasted. Knossos's magnificent frescoes were brilliant evidence of a highly developed artistic culture, including the world's first naturalistic depictions of landscape.

There was also an underground sewage system, the world's first known flush toilet, and extensive storage magazines, still filled with the signs of vast commercial wealth. Most exciting for Evans was the discovery of the prehistoric script now known as Linear B, which was vivid proof of an advanced, cultured society, the hub of Mediterranean Bronze Age civilization.

This was a landmark excavation. Newspapers across the world trumpeted the exciting news.

Evans's assistant Duncan Mackenzie kept detailed daily records, while Evans was tireless in documenting his research. Yet Evans's approach, while flamboyant and eye-catching, was hasty, viewed from a modern perspective. He shoehorned preconceived ideas into the mix in a desperate attempt to force the evidence into shape. Those distinctive, primitive-looking, black-topped red columns which are today the trademark of the site are built out of modern concrete and are part of Evans's "reconstruction". An educated guess, yes, but still a guess. Many years later it is hard to know what is original, and what is reconstructed. Scholars have to go back to the excavation records again and again to try and re-interpret what Evans and Mackenzie originally found, and where.

Minoan archaeology has come a long way since. What Evans desperately wanted to interpret as the magnificent royal residence of King Minos seems in truth to have been a religious shrine, or temple. Although Knossos may have had a highly powerful leader, he – or she – was most likely a religious figure, a kind of "Solar Moon King".

Ancient Minoans were just as often led by a priestess as a priest. Ironically, although he was the first to discover the enigmatic scripts known as Linear A and B, Evans was never able to translate them. He spent the rest of his life trying.

Could the Minoans be the inspiration behind the myth of the lost city of Atlantis? In a fascinating story of its own, a new wave of archaeological and geological evidence suggests that Minoan civilization was struck by a devastating tsunami that triggered huge destruction. It hit Crete after a volcanic eruption on the island of Thera (now Santorini), by then part of the greater Minoan maritime empire.

Relics of the
Roman Empire

It is impossible to encapsulate a full thousand years of Roman history in one short chapter, but the story of the Emperor Caracalla, best known for his magnificent public baths, which were free to all and even included a library, has a special resonance in today's world.

In 212 CE, Caracalla decreed that wherever they lived, from Spain to Syracuse, from the British Isles to Egypt, every free inhabitant of the Roman empire was a bona fide Roman citizen. Overnight, more than 30 million people from the provinces became legally Roman, which must qualify as the biggest offer of citizenship in world history.

To some eyes, this may seem strange, but the Romans had a unique way of appropriating the "other" as a way of preventing it from becoming dangerous. The cult of Cybele, an unexpected fruit of Rome's expansion into Anatolia, was initially thought to be a subversive, even menacing, form of worship. Yet the mother goddess's temple ended up on the Palatine, the very heart of Rome. Recent studies have shown that, far from looking to diminish the cult and its power, Rome's first emperor, Augustus, raised the floors of the temple and substantially restored it.

Foundations

In a city as well studied as this, it's surprising how much more there is to learn, but Rome never ceases to stun the world. According to legend, the twins Romulus and Remus founded Rome in the 8th century BCE. Romulus killed Remus in a dispute over which of them

THE RISE AND FALL OF THE ROMAN EMPIRE

753 BCE
Rome is founded
509 BCE
Rome becomes a republic
264 BCE
Rome completes the conquest
of Italy
183 BCE
Hannibal dies
73–71 BCE
Spartacus's Slave Rebellion
58–52 BCE
Julius Caesar conquers Gaul
46 BCE
Julius Caesar becomes
dictator
27 BCE
Augustus becomes emperor
27 BCE
The Roman empire begins

60/61 CE
Boudicca's Revolt
83 CE
Agricola completes conquest
of Britain
117 CE
The Roman empire is at its
height
212 CE
Freemen of the Roman
empire are given citizenship
325 CE
Constantine adopts
Christianity
410 CE
The Visigoths attack Rome
476 CE
The western Roman empire
ends and ancient Rome falls

had the support of the gods. Modern archaeological technologies are opening up many new discoveries: employing auger-type probes more often used in engineering, archaeologists even believe they have located the twins' very first home, the "Lupercal cave", deep in the honeycomb core of the Palatine Hill.

In the 19th century, Giacomo Boni rediscovered an ancient iron-age shrine, the Lapis Niger. In imperial Rome, it was said to be where Romulus met a grisly end, as members of the senate stabbed him to death. The records are unclear, but some describe the spot as a sacred part of the original Comitium, an early assembly place where rulers addressed the citizens.

Within the gloom of the buried temple, Boni found a mysterious inscribed stone, its writing running left to right, right to left, "as an ox would plough a field". This is the earliest Latin inscription ever found. No one has ever completely deciphered it, but one word does clearly stand out: "Rex" (king).

Augustus's famous Forum Romanum was built around and above this sacred space, which it has long been suspected holds the key to the foundation of Rome itself. Recently, a team of Italian archaeologists used laser scanners and photography from historical excavations to pinpoint the oldest walls underground, and employed modern techniques to re-date the minute fragments of pottery and grains in the surrounding level. The team feels their evidence pushes the story of the Eternal City, and possibly even that of Romulus and Remus, back by several hundred years.

The feats of engineering, together with the beauty, ingenuity and durability of the buildings that the Romans created still continue to amaze us. These were a major contribution to civic life. In the provinces, the well-ordered city was the prime agent in spreading Romanitas, a sense of Rome's benefits and its values.

In Rome, Caracalla's baths continued a long tradition of building on an imperial and lavish scale: the Circus Maximus; Hadrian's magnificent villa; the Colosseum, built to stamp out memories of Nero's lavish personal fun palace, and the "Golden House". Rome was a city of gold, marble and bronze, but its armies were tougher than old leather. Beyond its powerful walls and towers stretched the 1,931,000 miles^2 (5,000,000 km^2) of the empire. No one could have imagined that this great city would fall, but fall it did.

Two hundred years after Caracalla's death, in 410 CE, the Visigoths attacked and plundered the city. Over the centuries, the magnificent Forum became first a field where farmers grazed their cattle and grew vines, and then a swamp crawling with toads and vipers. Cows drank in the fountains, and the Colosseum's expensive dressed stone became a quarry for the popes. Rome echoed to the calls of the night birds across the banks of the filthy river Tiber.

Lost, but now found? A she-wolf is said to haveraised Rome's founding fathers in the Lupercal Cave.

Digital Rome

Rome is a multi-layered city, what scholars call a "palimpsest". For the first-time visitor, it can be a hard book to read. There's modern Rome, 18th-century Rome, Renaissance Rome. Then there's the Vatican, a city all to itself. And what of antiquity? The Emperor Augustus claimed to have turned this place from a city of brick into a city of marble; wouldn't it be wonderful to see the city as he did?

Since the Renaissance, artists, scholars, architects and – latterly – archaeologists have been trying to decipher the complex urban landscape of this city. Now, thanks to digital technology and a huge amount of dedicated scholarship, everyone can enjoy the fruits of their labour.

The Roman Antiquities Service (Forma Romae) is making it possible to explore the megalopolis through interactive maps or in virtual reality, via 3D models online. It is concentrating on Augustan Rome for now, although in future, it hopes to cover other periods. It aims to create accurate archaeoscapes that one can "fly" through.

How accurate a vision is this? Archaeology proves our interpretation of history can't be fixed, but the new virtual views of Rome are not video games; they are as well informed as it is possible to be. An American project from the universities of Arizona and Pennsylvania, Rome Reborn, focuses on specific aspects of the city, such as the magnificent Pantheon at the height of its glory. Dr Matthew Nicholls of the Classics Department at the University of Reading has created a digital model of the entire city – just as it would have been in the 4th century CE. In London, meanwhile, UCLA has created sophisticated digitized models with detailed "footnotes" on each building. One of the most impressive is a digital recreation of the Circus Maximus in the 4th century. This was the first and largest chariot-racing stadium in Rome, but was also used for *ludi*, huge religious festivals.

THE COLOSSEUM

The Colosseum showed the Romans at their mightiest but also at their most cruel. Built in 72–80 CE, the poet Martial described it as the eighth wonder of the world; the height of Roman building technology. The stadium could even be flooded to stage naval battles or redecorated as a jungle, to entertain up to 50,000 spectators. Behind those serried ranks of magnificent arches, the Romans killed thousands of people, many of them Christians. A favourite trick was to put prisoners on seesaws, and then release starving lions from the basement trapdoors. To survive, a prisoner had to drive his or her end of the seesaw into the air and be responsible for the person opposite being mauled and eaten. *Damnatio ad Bestius* – the Condemnation of Beasts.

The magnificent building illustrates one of the dilemmas of archaeology: how far to dig? Which period should you destroy, in order to restore another? Ironically, the Colosseum's use as a place of Christian martyrdom is one reason why it survived. In 1874, when archaeologists began to excavate, they removed a medieval hermit and his hermitage, along with the black Martyrs' cross seen immortalized in the engravings of Piranesi. Christians came out in protest, to pray on the sacred ground where the Martyrs had suffered and died. Nowadays, it is possible to see the extent of the hypogeum, the labyrinth of passageways and cages that existed beneath the arena.

Piranesi's engraving of the majestic building in which the Martyrs' cross can be seen in the middle.

Beyond Rome

Why was the Roman empire so successful, and how did it last for some 500 years? Sheer ingenuity played a large part. A map of the empire at the height of its territorial expansion under Trajan and Hadrian would show domination of most of modern Europe; the north coast of Africa including Egypt; much of Turkey and the Middle East, and a big slice of what is now Russia. Both Trajan and Hadrian were actually born in Spain.

Unity was achieved by tight initial control, using a universally accepted currency, and investing heavily in engineering works and infrastructure such as water works and roads. The Romans accepted the different customs, religions and cultures of the people they conquered, eventually making many of them citizens.

Rome offered remarkable modernity. Its mark can still be seen in language, laws, architecture, engineering and government. Many of the landmarks they created had a formal beauty and, like Leptis Magna or the Pont du Gard in France, are now listed by UNESCO as World Heritage sites. We are even now making major new Roman finds, like the city of Ucetia recently found at Uzès, in the south of France.

PUTTING UP A FIGHT: THE ROMANS IN BRITAIN

The Romans invaded Britain under Emperor Claudius. In 43 CE, the empire was only a few decades old, but entering a period of unparalleled expansion. Would a few obscure islands on the empire's north-western edges cause the super-efficient Romans any problems? Well, yes. While some British tribes were at odds with one another, which helped the Romans divide and rule, many put up stiff resistance, led at first by Togodumnus and Caratacus, sons of Cunobeline, king of the Catuvellauni.

Under Agricola's leadership between 78 and 84 CE, the Romans largely subdued the British, but rebellion against the invaders flared up repeatedly when he was recalled to Rome. Most notable was the revolt led by an alarmingly fierce, flame-haired Celt called Boudicca, queen of the Iceni.

Suetonius finally defeated Boudicca and her army at the Battle of Watling Street in 60 or 61 CE, but even so, Nero considered abandoning the Roman occupation of Britain altogether: too much trouble for too little gain. Boudicca's own fate is uncertain, although it's possible she took poison rather than surrender. For a society as patriarchal as ancient Rome, wrote the historian Dio, "the fact all this ruin was brought by a woman in itself caused them the greatest shame."

Fantastic tales abound that Boudicca is buried under platform 8, 9 or 10 in King's Cross Station. Burials from this time often leave no trace, especially when the death was in battle. Yet in 2012, as part of the London Crossrail project, archaeologists found a vast number of simultaneously buried skeletons. This added to intriguing evidence already found around the Roman Temple of Mithras in the City of London, which was only uncovered because of enemy bombing during World War II.

The temple was excavated in 1954 by William Grimes, whose work was rushed by development pressure. Winston Churchill stepped in and extended the excavation time, after thousands of people flocked to see the dig. Eventually, some of the finest Roman sculptures found in Britain were recovered.

The recent redevelopment of a 3-acre (1.2-hectare) site for Bloomberg became a chance to reconstruct the Temple of Mithras underneath the office block at the exact spot it was built in 240 CE. Ground level in Roman London was 23 ft (7 m) below today's. London's single largest archaeological excavation, it revealed a bustling Roman street scene from the 1st century CE, as well as the long-buried river Walbrook.

The dig uncovered a large ceramic pot containing some ritually buried skulls, gold coins, amulets and pagan tokens. All had been wonderfully preserved for almost 2,000 years in the muddy riverbed. It is tempting to think of Boudicca and her warriors sending these along the stream as offerings to the gods, much like the wonderful Battersea Shield. This beautifully worked Celtic, La Tène bronze shield was dredged out of the rich Thames mud in 1857; archaeologists believe it was a votive offering, and it too was found with the remains of many Roman-era skeletons.

BOUDICCA

Tacitus tells us that in 60 or 61 CE, the Romans flogged Boudicca and publicly raped both her daughters when she objected to the Roman annexation of Iceni lands – in present-day Norfolk. In response, Boudicca unleashed fury. The Iceni burned the Roman-occupied towns of Camulodunum (Colchester) and Londinium to the ground, killing thousands in the process. Clear burn lines in the stratigraphy attest to this. At Colchester, digs have shown that every care was taken to destroy everything that was Roman. Even buildings of clay, which is very difficult to burn, were demolished brick by brick. Every "collaborator" the Iceni could find was hunted down and killed: experts liken it to a campaign of ethnic cleansing. Boudicca may also have burned Verulamium (St Albans), although there is less clear archaeological evidence for this.

Vindolanda

The Vindolanda tablets give the best insight into what it was like to be a Roman citizen or soldier living in a fort on the very edge of the Roman empire. Hadrian's wall still separates England and Scotland. Before the wall was constructed, the earliest forts were entirely isolated. The first at Vindolanda was begun in 85 CE and finished by 92 CE. Most of the inscribed wooden tablets, which were ditched in a rubbish dump near the commander's mansio, or mansion, date from the period when the fort was enlarged, between 92 and 102 CE.

One tablet's dismissive description of the British makes it sound as if they remained an active enemy: "the Britons are unprotected by armour. There are very many cavalry. The cavalry does not use swords nor do the wretched little Britons mount in order to throw javelins." Yet many of the tablets give a sense of a relatively peaceful lifestyle. Perhaps the wall's primary purpose was not to keep out "savage barbarians", but to mark the limits of the empire as a political entity, and to levy taxes and customs duties?

In one well-known message, a centurion's wife, Claudia Severa, invites her sister, Lepidina, to a party. In another, an unknown soldier receives word of a care package: "I have sent you... pairs of socks from Sattua, two pairs of sandals and two pairs of underpants...." It sounds as if his mother – or his wife – was as worried about the British weather as she was about defending the wall.

The Bloomberg (Mithras) dig in London also unearthed an entirely new set of wooden tablets, even older than the ones at Vindolanda. Historically, one of the most important is a contract dated 22 October 62 CE for the transport of 20 wagonloads of provisions from St Albans to London. Tacitus dates Boudicca's rebellion to 61 CE, but if both St Albans and London were razed with enormous loss of life, it seems unlikely both cities could have bounced back quite so quickly. The tablet suggests that Boudicca's insurrection may well have taken place earlier. Whatever the exact truth, the separate forms of material, archaeological and historical evidence are an intriguing check and balance.

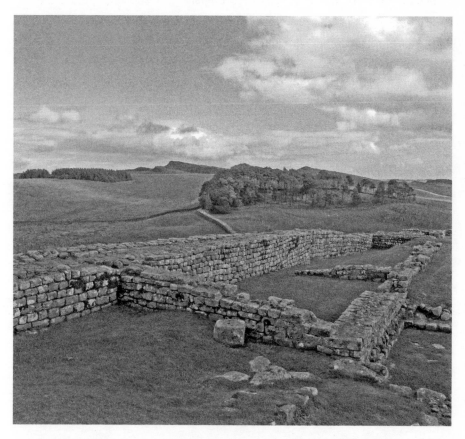

Remote Romans: Housesteads Roman fort, in the Northumbrian wilds.

The Bloomberg tablets prove that this area of London has been a trading and financial hub since the earliest years of the Roman occupation. There are 405 tablets in total, many of them recording financial transactions.

The western Roman empire effectively came to an end in the 5th century CE, but Roman influence in Britain had been on the wane for more than a century before that. However, the empire's remarkable legacy both in Britain and throughout Europe, North Africa and the Near East was incalculable.

Lords of the North

With the fall of the Roman empire, Europe entered a period of fragmentation, economic decline and frequent warfare known as the Dark Ages. As Roman authority collapsed, new powers rose to fill the vacuum. In northern Europe, the Norsemen of Scandinavia plundered, pillaged and colonized their neighbours at the same time as Christianity took root through much of the continent. Local kings and warlords sought to establish themselves as the natural successors to the fallen empire. Few written records from the period remain. To understand the world of the Vikings, we must turn to archaeology.

Raiders and Traders

Ragnar Hairy-breeks; Eric Bloodaxe; Ivar the Boneless; Eric the Red... the names read like a rogues' gallery, and with good reason. For while it may be true that the Vikings engaged in peaceful trading, loved a good story, worked metal brilliantly and were effective farmers, their record was also one of ruthless, murderous robbery. Until recently, both archaeologists and historians agreed that the raid on the holy island of Lindisfarne (in the north of England) in 793 CE marked the beginning of the Viking era. However, two Viking ship burials accidentally discovered in the course of cable laying on the Estonian island of Saaremaa in 2008 are challenging this theory. University of Tartu archaeologist Marge Konsa led the dig on the first boat, which held the remains of seven men aged between 18 and 45, together with their knives, whetstones and a bone comb. They had all died violently.

Radiocarbon dating of the boat timbers produced a surprising result: the vessel, which had no mast or sail, had been built between 650 and 700 – approximately 100 years before the Lindisfarne raid. The boat may have been used and repaired for decades prior to its final voyage.

Two years later, Jüri Peets from the University of Tallinn found a second, larger Viking ship nearby. As with the first, its timbers had rotted away; but the impression it had left in the soil and the position of the rivets and nails revealed that it was about 55 ft (17 m) long and 10 ft (3 m) wide. It had a keel, essential for seagoing, and Peets believes it also had a mast and a sail. If true, then Salme 2 is the oldest sailing vessel ever found in the Baltic.

The dead men were buried in a significant way: five warriors with richly decorated, double-edged swords had been positioned at the top of the pile. The bodies with cruder, single-edged weapons lay at the bottom. The hierarchical order suggests a raiding party led by an élite. One of the leaders – perhaps a king – had a decorated walrus-ivory gaming piece in his mouth. There were also mutton and beef bones and the remains of dogs. Were these pets, or attack dogs? The bones of a goshawk and a sparrowhawk were also found, most likely used for hunting game along the coast. Nobody knows whether these men were killed in an ill-fated raid on the island, or by rival Norse warriors. No matter how they died, the survivors buried them in haste. It is hoped isotope analysis can pinpoint their place of origin.

Bitter Enemies

Following the Lindisfarne raid, Viking raiding parties terrorized English shores, attacking villages along the coast and looting monasteries as they went. These were, however, just seasonal incursions – each winter they would return home to enjoy the spoils of the raiding season.

In 865 CE, this changed. A united coalition of Norse warriors, known as the "Great Heathen Army" by their Anglo-Saxon opponents, arrived on English shores intent on conquest. According to the Viking Sagas, the sons of Ragnar Lothbrok came on a mission of revenge, able to overcome their differences to subdue their English opponents. They would conquer the kingdoms of Northumbria, Mercia and East Anglia, with only Wessex avoiding their axe. Eventually, Alfred the Great stemmed the tide, defeating the Norsemen at Edington in 878 CE – but the respite was only temporary. B

eginning in 1974, Martin Biddle and Birthe Kjølbye-Biddle excavated the site of St Wystan's Church at Repton, in Derbyshire. Referenced in the *Anglo-Saxon Chronicle*, the town was the winter base of the "Great Army" between 873 and 874 CE. They found a body buried with a piece of jewellery representing Thor's Hammer, with wounds on the skull and spine. Nearby, they found the remains of at least 250 more individuals, plus a central coffin containing what is (ironically) believed to be the skeleton of the legendary Viking warrior, Ivar the Boneless.

Mass graves found across the UK detail the conflict between Norseman and Anglo-Saxon. At Ridgeway, near Weymouth, a grave containing 54 skeletons, dating back to approximately 1000 CE, was discovered in 2009. Isotope evidence showed the bodies were of Scandinavian origin – evidence of a Viking raiding party that came to a bloody end.

KING ARTHUR

Did King Arthur really exist? The legend of the Briton who led the defence against the Saxon invaders of the fifth and sixth centuries is compelling, but actual evidence for the tale popularized by the fanciful accounts of the medieval cleric Geoffrey of Monmouth is sparse. Brief mentions of the famous leader in the Venerable Bede's *Ecclesiastical History of the English People* and in the *Historia Brittonum* have added little to the factual database. According to legend, Tintagel in Cornwall was the birthplace of King Arthur. Pottery dating to the era was first discovered at the site by Raleigh Radford in the 1930s, but it has only been more recently that major archaeological investigations have been undertaken. In 1998, a stone inscribed with the name "Artognou" was discovered there and sparked speculation that the first evidence for the legendary leader was about to be uncovered. In 2016, the Cornwall Archaeological Unit, in association with English Heritage, unearthed the walls of a 6th-century palace. The team found more than 150 fragments from glass and pottery vessels, suggesting active international trade. Earthwork surveys showed evidence of 100 buildings. Whether this was truly the home of the legendary King Arthur or "merely" a royal palace of the Kingdom of Dumnonia, the excavations underway at Tintagel continue to reveal secrets about the so-called Dark Ages.

Overseas Adventures

The Vikings travelled far and wide from their Scandinavian homelands. Archaeologists have found extensive evidence of their presence in France, Italy, the Iberian peninsula and Russia. Dr Irene García Losquiño has investigated a number of anchors that washed up on a beach in Galicia. Nearby was a Viking-constructed mound called a *longphort* that closely resembled Viking camps found in Ireland and England. The Vikings' presence in Iberia has received little attention from archaeologists in the past. That is now beginning to change.

Meanwhile, at Staraya Ladoga in western Russia, evidence of a 9th-century Viking settlement was uncovered in 1997, including Scandinavian jewellery and a burned-down Viking workshop. In nearby Dalnaja bay, a longship dating to the 10th century was also found. The largest Viking archaeological site in Russia is at Gnezdovo, located on the Dnieper River near Smolensk. Excavation of the site, which consists of 3,000 burial mounds, began in 1867, when a hoard of silver jewellery was first uncovered. Many of the items demonstrate a pronounced Viking presence, from jewellery to weaponry, but Byzantine and Arabic coins also show the importance of the site as an important part of an international trading system. The Slavs and Greeks described the Vikings as "Varangians", who sailed the river systems of Russia, raiding and trading just as they did elsewhere in Europe. Eventually, a group of these Norsemen settled in the region and formed the basis of Kievan Rus. It was through Russia that the Vikings made their way to Greece and the most spectacular city of medieval Europe, Constantinople. There, the names of two Vikings are carved with runes on a marble balcony at Hagia Sophia (the former church and mosque, now a museum).

The Splendours of the Dark Ages

Archaeological treasures abound in the world of the Dark Ages. From Anglo-Saxon hoards containing intricate jewellery and gleaming coins to Viking settlements across the Atlantic, archaeological discoveries are revealing a world connected by trade, warfare and cultural exchange that makes the term "Dark Ages" an ugly misnomer. In a time of few written records, the material remains of these cultures has been incredibly revealing. Ongoing excavations at Tintagel, Galicia and Gnezdovo continue to uncover the Viking Age and distinguish myth from reality.

L'ANSE AUX MEADOWS

The 11th-century Viking settlement of L'Anse aux Meadows in Newfoundland, Canada, proves Norsemen discovered North America long before Christopher Columbus. Excavations of "Leif's Camp", named after Leif Erikson, who first made landfall there around 1000 CE, have revealed longhouses and workshops built in the same style and with the same methods as buildings from the same period in Greenland and Iceland, as well as evidence of contemporary Scandinavian iron-working. Archaeologists are investigating a second possible Viking site at Port Rosée, 300 miles (483 km) south of L'Anse aux Meadows.

THE SEA KINGS

With a commanding view of the River Deben, the open, estuary site of Sutton Hoo speaks of a high-living culture that used the sea, rather than the land, as its Silk Road.

One summer night on the eve of World War II, Edith Pretty looked out of the window and saw a series of ghostly, warlike figures in armour walking across the fields outside. She rushed to the nearest museum in Ipswich, which recommended a local, self-taught archaeologist named Basil Brown to investigate the lozenge-shaped mounds around her property. Brown began work in 1938 and decided to tackle the largest, Mound 1. What he found changed British archaeology forever Inside was the impressed shape of buried longboat, and the grave good of a great Saxon king, Raedwald. I was an entire ocean-going wooder vessel, 88 ft (27 m) long, rivets still in position.

When the Angles, Saxons, Jutes and Frisians invaded Britain, during the 5th and 6th centuries CE, the area conquered slowly became known as Angleland (England). Their several kingdoms, constantly at war with one

The charismatic Sutton Hoo helmet, perhaps the most striking of the many treasures unearthed at the site.

another, sometimes acknowledged one of their rulers as the Bretwalda, or "High King". Straddling the margin between myth and history, Raedwald was one of these.

Within the ship was an extraordinary treasure trove which demonstrated that this culture had extraordinary levels of sophistication and artistic skill. It contained a sceptre; magnificent gold-and-garnet cloisonné jewellery including ornate garnet and gold shoulder clasps; a stock of domestic items for use in the next world; and a majestic, pattern-welded sword, its scabbard inlaid with intricate crosses and mushroom shapes. Crowning it all was a remarkable iron and bronze war helm and a huge boss shield. The helmet is one of only five known, and is extravagantly and delicately worked.

With cloaks from Syria, silver from Byzantium and bowls from Africa, the finds at Sutton Hoo proved that this was a thriving, commercially confident culture with a truly continental outlook.

BASIL BROWN (1888–1977)

In 1929 Basil John Wait Brown discovered and excavated the 7th-century Anglo-Saxon ship burial at Sutton Hoo in Suffolk.

Born in 1888, Brown's family moved to a farm near Rickinghall, in Suffolk, the district where he would spend most of his life. His interest in astronomy and excavation began early. He was sent to Rickinghall School but left at the age of 12 to work on his father's farm. Through his own efforts, evening courses and correspondence courses, he educated himself in astronomy, geography and geology, teaching himself Latin and French with some knowledge of Greek, German and Spanish.

In the 1920s and 30s Brown continued his interest in astronomy, publishing articles and a book. In his spare time, he investigated the countryside near his home for Roman remains, uncovering eight medieval buildings, identifying Roman settlements, and tracing ancient roads. Through Guy Maynard, curator of the Ipswich Museum, he was employed on a contractual basis to carry out a number of excavations including at Stanton Chare where he discovered a Roman villa. Although this work provided him with some income he was obliged to work as an insurance agent and special constable as well.

When, in the summer of 1938, Edith Pretty wanted to find out more about the contents of the ancient mounds on her

Sutton Hoo estate, she was introduced to Guy Maynard who offered the services of Basil Brown as excavator at a rate of 30 shillings a week. With an initial time-limit of two weeks, Brown decided to copy cross-trench digging methods that had been used in 1934 excavations of Iron Age mounds at Warborough Hill in Norfolk.

With the help of labourers employed by Edith Pretty, Brown excavated three mounds, discovering that they were burial sites that showed signs of robbery during the medieval period. He also found a number of pottery shards, ship's rivets and the shape of a boat which appeared to have been cut in half, as well as a gold-plated shield boss, and glass fragments.

In August 1938 Brown went back to work for the Ipswich Museum, returning to the dig at Stanton Chare. The following year, at Pretty's request, Brown returned to the site at Sutton Hoo for a second season. On 8 May 1939 he started to excavate Mound 1, the largest mound. On 11 May he found iron rivets similar but larger to those found in Mound 2, suggesting an even larger sailing vessel than the boat found previously. Brown then found an impression left in the soil by a ship 27 m (88 ft) long. It appeared that robbers had stopped before they had reached the level of a burial deposit. Based on their knowledge of ship burials in Norway, Brown and Guy Maynard thought it very likely that a roof had covered the burial chamber.

On 6 June Charles Phillips of Selwyn College, Cambridge visited the site. He suggested that the British Museum and the Ancient Monuments Department of the Ministry of Works should be informed and he was subsequently given control over excavations, starting in July. Basil Brown was allowed to continue with his work, and uncovered the burial chamber on

14 June, followed later by the ship's stern. Although Brown continued to work on the site in accordance with his contract with Pretty, he was excluded from excavating the burial chamber that he had located.

Although often described as an amateur archaeologist, Brown was employed by the Ipswich Museum as a paid excavator for more than 30 years. Although he did not publish on his archaeological findings as a sole author, his notebooks, including photographs, plans and drawings are held by the Suffolk County Council Archaeological Service, leading to the establishment of the County Sites and Monuments Record of Suffolk which still exists today.

The Archaeology
of the
Americas

Rewriting the
History Books

In North America, until the last five centuries, human history went unrecorded. With no written record, on this continent archaeology has been crucial to understanding the past. Pioneers such as Cyrus Thomas and Frederic Putnam slowly revealed the rich cultural identity hidden under the surface.

Who were the earliest Americans, and how and when did they get there? Until recently it was thought that there were no people on the continent at all before 14,000 years ago. New archaeological discoveries are now pushing back the clock. The Americas were the last great land mass to be colonized by humanity. How, why and when did people first arrive?

The planet was cold, and vast sheets of ice lay over most of North America, locking up so much of the world's water that sea levels were around 400 ft (120 m) lower than they are today. Vast stretches of ocean floor opened up and islands stopped being islands, and became peninsulas. People may have made their way south around 13,000 years ago, across the land bridge that once existed between Alaska and Russia. Much of this prehistoric valley – now known as "Beringia", after the Bering Straits – is underwater.

Above the Bluefish River in northern Yukon sit a series of limestone caves that have caused a stir in the archaeological community. In the 1970s, Jacques Cinq-Mars studied the many animal remains left in the caves for proof of human activity. New radiocarbon dating techniques now prove beyond reasonable doubt that humans lived in or visited the cave system at least 24,000 years ago, at the height of the last Ice Age. One horse jaw bone in particular shows evidence of distinct human cut marks.

Assuming the land bridge theory is correct, were the people who crossed it the same as the "Clovis people" whom archaeologists once thought were the first to inhabit the Americas? "Clovis points" are beautifully carved stone arrowheads. Slender and fluted, they have been found all over North America, including the Beringia area. But there is a new twist in the tale: archaeologists are currently finding evidence at different dig sites – for example at Schaefer Farm, an hour north of Chicago – that other groups, with older tool technologies were around well before the people who made the Clovis points. Their presence would suggest the Beringia theory is wrong.

Delicate but deadly:
Clovis points.

A controversial 2017 study seeks to turn this thesis on its head. New radiocarbon results show a mastodon skeleton discovered by palaeontologists in San Diego in 1992 is 130,000 years old. It was discovered near a collection of stone tools – which had presumably been used to kill and skin it – from the Late Pleistocene period. The discovery is rewriting our understanding of the spread of the human species across the globe. If the clear cut marks plainly seen on its limbs were made by humans, then this implies that humans – or more precisely the predecessors of *Homo sapiens* – arrived in the Americas more than 100,000 years before anyone had previously believed.

As the Bering Sea hurls storms of new violence against the coast, the permafrost will erode away. This process of climate change could soon bring new revelations about the peopling of the Americas. The warmer temperatures are already revealing new layers of past history – for instance at the settlement of Nunalleq, the big melt is revealing evidence hidden in the ground for four-and-a-half centuries. The site shows that the Little Ice Age of the 1600s caused wars between different bands of Yupik. An entire settlement of 50 people appears to have been smoked out of their sod hut and slaughtered, probably for their food.

Mastodon molars: clear evidence of cut marks.

THE KENNEWICK MAN CONTROVERSY

In 1996, two students made a remarkable discovery in the
Columbia River in Kennewick, Washington: a skeleton
that was almost 9,000 years old. Will Thomas was getting
ready to watch the town's annual boat race. He spotted what
looked like a skull sticking out of the water. Thinking it was
a boulder, Thomas decided to play a trick on his friend. He
reached into the water and pulled the object free. It was
indeed a human skull. Kennewick Man's skeleton was almost
entirely intact, a rare occurrence. The discovery began a
controversy that would last more than two decades. Local
Native American tribes wanted the body of the man they
described as "The Ancient One" returned to them under
the Native American Graves Protection and Repatriation
Act (NAGPRA). The archaeologist who had first carbon-
dated Kennewick Man's skeleton, James Chatters, and the
Smithsonian's forensic expert Douglas Owsley believed
the bones were not genetically related to modern Native
Americans. Physically, he resembled Polynesian peoples more.
The court case lasted nine years. More than two decades after
its discovery, on 18 February 2017, a coalition of Columbia
Basin tribes reburied the body.

A Forgotten World

Impressive sites like Serpent Mound, Chaco Canyon and the Verde
Valley show that Native American civilizations were far more
complex than their European colonizers first believed. In the wild
1860s, the first groups of miners, soldiers and explorers arrived in

central Arizona's Verde Valley. About 100 ft (34 m) above Beaver Creek, they found a dramatic 20-room, multi-storey dwelling built up into a sheer limestone cliff. It was obvious that the structure had been abandoned for a very long time, and the stone floors were covered with bat lime.

The newcomers dubbed the structure "Montezuma's Castle", reasoning that such building skills must have been Aztec, not Native American. The "Castle" was built by the Sinagua people, close relatives of the Hohokam people who dominated the ancient Southwest.

Archaeological evidence suggests a sequence of settlements, beginning around 900 CE, was interrupted by a volcanic eruption. Despite its sophistication, by 1425, the Verde Valley site had been abandoned: but no one knows quite why.

It is so high up that its inhabitants must have used rope ladders to make their precarious way into their homes. In the 1870s, Colonel Hiram C. Hodge only managed to reach it by "clinging to poles and jutting points of rock".

It is estimated that some 50 people could have lived here at a time. Archaeological discoveries in the lower section of the valley show the "castle" type of structure was the exception, not the rule: by 1300, most of the estimated 6–8,000 people then present in the area were living in small villages on the valley bottom. A large amount of what we do know about the people comes from the less spectacular "Castle A" nearby, which was spared the large-scale looting from which the more picturesque "Montezuma" suffered.

In 1906, President Theodore Roosevelt proclaimed "Montezuma Castle" a national monument. This was the first prehistoric ruin in the US to be protected under the 1906 Antiquities Act. The looting had finally been stopped.

FREDERIC WARD PUTNAM (1839–1915)

Putnam – sometimes known as "The Father of American Archaeology" – was the archaeologist responsible for developing two of the most respected anthropological departments in the United States – at Harvard University and the University of California, Berkeley. He also developed the Peabody Museum, the American Museum of Natural History, Chicago's Field Museum of Natural History and Berkeley's Anthropological Museum. He was active in the field, too. He made several excavations at Serpent Mound in southern Ohio between 1880 and 1895. Putnam dedicated much of his life to saving a place that inspired him "with a singular sensation of awe". Encouraging private donations from "a group of Boston ladies", he and the historian Francis Parkman bought the site and turned it into a public park. In 1991, a team of archaeologists reopened one of Putnam's original trenches, finding bits of charcoal that are now possible to date via Carbon-14 dating. Tests indicated the mound's most likely builders were the "Fort Ancient" villagers from c.10–15,000 BCE.

Born and raised in Salem, Massachusetts, Putnam studied both at private schools, and at home with his father. He was appointed curator of ornithology at the Essex Institute in

A map of Serpent
Mound, produced for
the book, *From Ancient
Monuments to the
Mississippi*, a landmark
publication by journalist
Ephraim Squier and Dr
Edwin Davis in 1848.

Salem in 1856 while still in his teens but a meeting with the
biologist Louis Agassiz led to Putnam studying with him at
Lawrence Scientific School of Harvard University. He fell out
with Agassiz over the theory of evolution and led his fellow
students in an academic revolt. Graduating from Harvard
in 1862, he worked with fellow students Edward Sylvester
Morse, A. S. Packard and Alpheus Hyatt and all four became
the founders of the periodical *American Naturalist* in 1867.
Putnam originated *The Naturalist's Directory* in 1865.

Putnam became the first director of the Peabody Museum
of Salem in 1864, having helped to convince George Peabody
to put up the money to found the museum. Three years
later he became superintendent of the East Indian Marine
Society's Museum at Salem. His archaeological interest
could be dated from the publication in 1865, of a paper
titled: "An Indian Grave and its Contents, on Winter Island,

Salem, Massachusetts." From thereon, his interest seems to have switched to focus almost exclusively on archaeology. In 1874 he became the curator of the Peabody Museum of Archaeology and Ethnology at Harvard University, a position he held for the next 25 years.

He also directed archaeological digs, eventually working across 37 US states as well as in other countries. When, in 1875 he was employed as civilian assistant on the United States surveys west of the 100th meridian, his duties were to investigate and report on the archaeological and ethnological material collected. His archaeological survey of Ohio from 1880–95 saw him focus his attention on ensuring the preservation of the Great Serpent Mound.

Appointed the lead curator and head of the anthropology department in 1891 for the World's Columbian Exposition, to be held in Chicago in 1893, he organized expeditions dispatched throughout the Americas and the wider world to gather natural history and ethnographic items. When the exhibition was coming to an end, he lobbied to find a permanent home for the collection of objects that had been put together, resulting, late in 1893, in the incorporation of the Field Museum of Natural History.

Mound Builders

The sophisticated city of Cahokia was a medieval Manhattan, peopled by many First Nation tribes. By 1050, this Mississippian metropolis was a major centre of some 30,000 people; yet, by 1350, it had been abandoned. Why? The city covered 9 miles^2 (23.3 km^2) with 120 earthen mounds inside its borders, and appears to have been a spiritual magnet, drawing people from afar. The largest structure, known as Monk's Mound, was a colossus made up of more than 22 million ft³ (623,000 m³) of soil. It must have taken the labour of thousands, as the lawyer Henry Brackenridge wrote to his friend Thomas Jefferson.

The city lay at the centre of a nationwide trading network that stretched as far as the Greak Lakes and the Gulf coast. Its inhabitants lived well-fed lives and cultivated goosefoot and amaranth, as well as corn. They also smelted copper. Cahokia's 2-mile- (3.2-km) long palisade was surrounded by hundreds of thatched homes with wooden post walls. The people linked their quarters with courtyards, plazas, pathways and roads and lived cheek by jowl with a constant stream of incomers. Strontium tests on teeth have found that at least a third of the population was from elsewhere in America.

Twentieth-century development took a terrible toll on Cahokia, with one mound entirely destroyed by farming, and the place being used variously as a gambling hall and even a pornographic drive-in. President Dwight Eisenhower's interstate highway programme finally paid the bill for archaeologists to investigate sites in its path, and put Cahokia on the map.

A university team from Wisconsin-Milwaukee began mapping the site in 1966. They soon discovered that Cahokia had been built very suddenly in what they now call a "Big Bang". Yet the mysterious abandonment question has still not been answered. Tim Pauketat at the University of Illinois believes that Cahokia controlled outlying villages and that they supplied tributes to élites within the city.

The discovery of one mound with sinister mass burials, most of young women, suggests that ritual human sacrifice may have been practised.

THE MYSTERY OF HOCHELAGA

Canada's first excavation, led by McGill University's John Dawson, was a fruitless search for the mysterious Hochelaga. This First Nation settlement was originally described by French explorer Jacques Cartier after an expedition in 1535. Yet by 1603, the entire village had completely disappeared. Recent building development in modern-day Montreal was halted when photographer Robert Galbraith realized that the bulldozers would intrude on the edge of the site that Dawson had excavated. Cartier had described a palisaded settlement with bark-covered houses, but Dawson found no evidence of a village as large. It is possible Cartier introduced devastating disease to the indigenous Iroquois, or the settlement was in fact a temporary fishing station. The practice of quick-moving settlements is not unique to Canada's Iroquois. In Newfoundland, L'Anse aux Meadows was only occupied for a few years. Archaeologist Sarah Parcak has recently identified another Canadian Viking site hundreds of miles south, at Point Rosée. Her news, of Nordic-style long barns and the hearth-stones that indicate iron-working, would seem to confirm the ancient Norse sagas of Erik the Red and the Greenlanders. Columbus was not the first European to discover – and explore – the North American continent.

Space Exploration

Driven by romantic notions of pioneers and patriots, US archaeology really got into its stride in the 1930s at colonial sites like Jamestowne. Nevertheless, archaeologists had already challenged absurd 19th-century justifications for eradicating American Indian populations. Rigorous excavation allowed the Smithsonian ethnologist-turned-archaeologist Cyrus Thomas to dismiss the "vanished race" theory that held that almost anyone except Native American Indians could have been the mound builders.

The main drive in the discipline today is towards inclusivity and collaboration. Sub-fields developing in US historical archaeology include specialisms in factory staff, plantation slaves and Chinese labourers.

Neither is the field a stranger to innovation, largely led by digitization. Academic Sarah Parcak, winner of the $1 million TED Prize in 2016, is even planning to create a cutting-edge "global alarm system" to identify and protect ancient sites from being looted. The work would be crowd-sourced among volunteers. Parcak describes herself as a "space archaeologist": she is the world's foremost specialist in making modern-day treasure maps – with satellite imagery. Using the vantage point of space, Parcak spots subtle signatures in the soil or in vegetation that are caused by unusual buried structures. Perhaps, she says, the future of archaeology lies in not digging things up. In 20 or 30 years, we may stop excavating entirely, and send in unobtrusive nano-robots to explore the hidden world underground.

Historic Jamestowne

The story of the "lost fort" at America's first European settlement had fascinated American archaeologists for decades, but its location continued to elude them. An excavation by the National Park Service had turned up nothing. Dr William Kelso believed they were looking in the wrong place. Convinced that the 17th-century brick church tower was a part of the original fort, he soon found evidence of pottery fragments and weapons in the area, hinting that his educated guess was correct.

In 1994, the Jamestown Rediscovery Project was launched after extensive preliminary work and negotiations with Preservation Virginia. More than 20 years later, the team has located not just the fort and the original settlement, but the remains of some of the founders themselves – along with artefacts that speak volumes about their lives. By 2010, they had located the site of the first church. There, they discovered the graves of the founders of the first permanent British settlement in America. Excavators uncovered a body buried with a captain's staff, which was only carried by British officers, suggesting it was Captain Gabriel Archer. High-resolution CT scans revealed the silver box found resting on the coffin was a Catholic reliquary, complete with a crucifix and holy oils. This in itself was a revelation, as Archer had ostensibly been leading a band of devout Protestants. The other bodies were identified through multiple lines of evidence, including chemical analyses, 3D imaging and their teeth. They were the Rev. Robert Hunt, Sir Ferdinando Wainman and Captain William West.

Those who had been in the New World the longest had extensive tooth decay and abscesses: corn leaves a sugary residue, which is much worse for your teeth than the barley and wheat-based diet of Europe. Nevertheless, they would have been grateful for that corn: during the "starving time" – a six-month period following their arrival – 250 people perished.

Ultimately, Jamestown only survived with the help of Powhatan, chief of the Powhatan Indians of Tidewater. Another long-term excavation project in Virginia, of a Monacan village, is revealing a more complex picture. Project leader Jeffrey Hantman of the University of Virginia wants to examine why Powhatan opted to side with the settlers. Artefacts which Hantman has found so far suggest that Powhatan was dependent for his wealth on trading copper. In trading his corn for John Smith's copper, he gained the upper hand on his Monacan rivals.

Today, "Historic Jamestowne" is a beacon example of a visit-friendly excavation. It is well worth exploring its website; you can watch the digging or even book a tour with the Director of Archaeology, Dr William Kelso.

POCAHONTAS

You might think that Pocahontas was a legend – but not
only did she exist, hers is also a genuine tale of crossing
cultures. A member of the indigenous Powhatan tribe, the
real Pocahontas brought food to the first, starving settlers
of Jamestown; and by marrying one of them, John Rolfe, she
also effected an uneasy peace. When she was 21, Pocahontas
visited England where she met King James II – and contracted
the tuberculosis that killed her.

Cultural
Giants

In Mesoamerica and South America, civilizations flourished before the arrival of Columbus. When the Spanish invaders arrived, they found cities larger than anything they had seen in Europe, beautiful architecture, complex social structures and elaborate religious rituals. The conquest of the Aztec and Inca empires and the subsequent desire to consolidate Spanish rule meant that the authorities sought to suppress these cultures. The great civilizations of the Americas faded into the background until adventurous travellers and amateur archaeologists began to uncover the extensive history that lay beneath their feet.

Despite 100 years of research, archaeologists have only scratched the surface of the history buried under the huge land mass of South America. New technology is beginning to re-write the history of its early cultures, in particular the million-dollar LiDAR scanners that can probe laser light through remote jungle from the air.

From 1200 BCE onwards, the precocious Olmec culture created Mesoamerica's first great art style on Mexico's Gulf Coast, with its mysterious monumental, 9-ft (3-m)-high, sculpted heads of rulers. Soon the complex Mayan city-states arose further south, whose stone reliefs mark key events in the lives of their kings and queens. On Peru's Pacific north coast, Caral may have been the first urban complex in the Americas.

In highland Mexico, by 600 CE, Teotihuacan housed as many as 200,000 inhabitants, one of the six largest urban centres of its time. It was one of the first sites to be excavated in the Americas. During the late 17th century, Carlos de Siguenza y Góngora, a creole priest

One of the giant heads of the Olmec rulers, which date from before 900 BCE. Each head has a distinctive headdress.

and poet born in New Spain, dug around the Pyramid of the Sun at Teotihuacan. He advanced the theory that the indigenous Mexicans were actually descendants of Egyptians.

Serious archaeological investigation of Teotihuacan began in the early 20th century with the work of Porfirio Díaz Leopoldo Batres. The magnificent ziggurats of the city were the earliest examples of public architecture, attempts to control the invisible forces of nature that govern the success or failure of crops. There are no towers or defences at abandoned Teotihuacan, the model metropolis, but we do know that sacrifice, both animal and human, took place in front of thousands of spectators. Sacred sites and temples such as the kalasasaya (sacred enclosure) at Tiwanaku and the Templo Mayor (great temple) at Tenochtitlan are meticulously planned around key sunrises and sunsets in the calendar.

EMPIRES OF THE AMERICAS

▼ ANDES

3500–1800 BCE
Norte Chico
100 BCE–800 CE
Nazca
100–800
Moche
300–1150
Tiwanaku
500–1000
Wari
900–1476
Chimu
1476–1534
Inca

▼ MEXICO

1200–400 BCE
Olmec
c.1–650 CE
Teotihuacan
400 BCE–1521 CE
Zapotec
900–1168
Toltec
1428–1521
Mexica (Aztec)

Ruins Beneath the Roads

The Aztec empire developed extensive trade networks in symbolically powerful materials such as the shimmering, iridescent feathers of the quetzal bird. It promoted a militaristic state ideology.

Beneath the busy roads of Mexico City lies the ancient city of Tenochtitlan. For years, the Aztec capital languished forgotten beneath the modern capital. Then in 1978, electrical workers laying cables accidentally came across the Aztec Templo Mayor. They found a monolith with a relief of Coyolxauhqui. Eduardo Matos Moctezuma directed the excavation of the site between 1978 and 1982. More than 7,000 objects were uncovered, revealing that this was the religious centre of the Aztec empire and one of the most important archaeological sites in the world. It covered an area of almost 43,000 ft² (4,000 m²).

Since the discovery of the Templo Mayor, a serious attempt has been made to uncover the city's material past. Archaeological excavations are underway throughout the city, from the basements of tattoo parlours to subway stations to the floor of the Metropolitan Cathedral. Archaeologists in Mexico City face special challenges – the teeming, packed city requires them carefully to navigate around sewers, pipes and subway lines. Flooding of the sites is also a problem.

THE LOST CITY OF THE MONKEY GOD

Tales of the legendary "La Ciudad Blanca" or "The White City" were told of a lost city hidden deep inside the rainforest in the Mosquitia region of Honduras. Hernán Cortés had heard the rumours, but never found the city. The aviator

Charles Lindbergh reported in 1927 seeing a white city while flying over eastern Honduras. In 1939, Theodore Morde claimed to have found a "City of the Monkey God" that fitted the description, but he died before he could explore it extensively. More than 200 sites have been documented in the region, most dating from between 800 and 1250 CE, but few have been properly investigated. Beginning in 2009, the film maker Steve Elkins began the Under the LiDAR project to find the Lost City once and for all. He and his team discovered an ancient city in the Honduran rainforest. An entire culture, separate from the nearby Maya, had been discovered. They found artefacts ranging from ceremonial seats to pottery carved with snakes and vultures to the head of a "were-jaguar". And archaeologists believe there may be more lost cities lying hidden in the Central American rainforest.

Imperial Ambitions in Peru

The earliest civilization in Peru was that of the Norte Chico, which at its height in the 3rd millennium BCE included as many as 30 cities. At the time, it was one of the most densely populated areas of the world. Aspero was the first site to be investigated. In 1941, two Harvard academics, Gordon R. Willey and John M. Corbett, found a building with no pottery, a few maize cobs and a number of artificial mounds. Years later, a graduate student used radiocarbon dating to test the samples – he found they originated in 3000 BCE – a date so much earlier than any other comparable site in the Americas he believed he had made a mistake. But in 1994, similar results were uncovered throughout the area by Ruth Shady Solis from the National University of San Marcos in Lima. She began excavating

Caral, a site she dated to 2600 BCE. A city at Huaricanga was dated to 3500 BCE, and sites at Porvenir and Upaca dated to 2700 BCE. The findings here led American archaeologists Winifred Creamer and Jonathan Haas to advance the MFAC hypothesis – the maritime foundations of Andean civilization. These sites had depended upon fishery, not agriculture. In this way, they were utterly different from the early civilizations that emerged in the Fertile Crescent, China and India.

One of the great mysteries of Peruvian archaeology are the Nazca lines. In the Nazca desert, huge lines have been carved into the landscape, making 300 geometric figures and 70 animal and plant designs. Some of the lines are as long as 30 miles (48 km). Their sheer scale means that it is difficult to observe them except from the air. They were made by the Nazca culture that ruled the area between 100 BCE and 800 CE. Archaeologists have been unable to discover the purpose behind these lines, but some theorize

Beautifully detailed, this is one of a pair of earflares made by the Moche. Earflares were large, circular adornments, popular among Peruvian lords as a sign of status and wealth.

that they were used for ritual and ceremonial purposes to pray to the gods for water.

For more than a millennium, tons of rock and brick had preserved priceless treasure buried deep inside a pyramid on the Peruvian north coast. The Moche civilization pre-dated the Incas by some 1,000 years and was first identified by archaeologist Max Uhle. Their distinctive Mochica pots can be found in museums the world over, looted from their context in ancient sites. The Moche had survived in one of the world's most arid regions by developing a technologically complex network of aqueducts and irrigation canals.

The Inca created the largest native state in the Americas of 10 million subjects, expanding with remarkable rapidity from their homeland in the Cuzco Valley to rule over a vast swathe of Andean South America. In the Quito area, 37 forts have been identified, defending strategic passes and routes. The most impressive Inca archaeological site is at Machu Picchu. The Incas captured the sacred objects of their enemies and symbolically imprisoned them in their Coricancha temple/fortress at Cuzco that was dedicated to Quilla, the goddess of the moon. The temple was covered in silver, thought to be the tears of moonlight. Coricancha, or The Golden Enclosure, was the centre of the Inca world. In the great temple of Inti, the golden walls were studded with emeralds. Their star religious icon, the golden statue of Inti, was taken to a place of safety when the Spanish arrived, but has never been found again.

MAX UHLE (1856–1944)

Though born in Germany, Max Uhle made notable contributions to the understanding of ancient cultures in South America. He was born in the east German city of Dresden, receiving a PhD from the University of Leipzig in 1880. He formed a great interest in Peru when employed as a curator at Dresden Museum. A few years later, Uhle's friend Alphons Stübel, who also had a deep knowledge of the region and had written on its archaeology, suggested that Uhle concentrate his studies there. He went to South America in 1892 to begin research in Argentina and Bolivia on behalf of the Ethnological Museum of Berlin. That same year, in partnership with photographer and engineer Georges B. von Grumbkow he published *The Ruins of Tiahuanaco in the Highlands of Ancient Peru*, thought to be the first scientific account of that site and notable for the comprehensive nature of its approach.

He returned again to South America in 1896, with sponsorship from the American Exploration Society of Philadelphia, as well as Mrs Phoebe Hearst, the mother of the newspaper magnate William Randolph Hearst. His excavations took him to Pachacamac, near the coast of Peru, and to sites at Mochica and Chimu. His site report from Pachacamac is still used as a starting text for studying South American archaeology. Uhle recognized versions of images he had seen on stone sculptures at Tiahuanaco on ceramics, textiles, and other artefacts at the coastal sites.

On this occasion, he unearthed some 9,000 artefacts covering more than 3,000 years of Andean pre-history. The items included Nazca pottery, shells, textiles, metals, objects of wood and other plant material, and those made of feathers, bone, and leather. He established a dating system based on changes in the design of textiles, while items found in the Mocha Valley were dated according the sequential position of Inca ceramic styles. This early dating was further developed by American archaeologist Alfred Kroeber and has become essential to the understanding of the chronology of pre-Inca Peru. Max Uhle subsequently led excavations in the highlands of Bolivia, Ecuador and Chile and in 1917 he became the first person to produce a scientific description of the Chinchorro mummies.

In 1926, about 12 km(7.5 miles) east of Quito, Ecuador, with palaeontologist Franz Spillmann, he excavated an almost entire mastodon skeleton, along with obsidian and bone tools and about 150 pieces of pottery. Uhle also excavated the Emeryville shell-mound in San Francisco Bay, California.

THE LORD OF SIPÁN

South America's cultural patrimony has been plundered for hundreds of years. Peruvian archaeologist Walter Alva saved the spectacular tomb of the Lord of Sipán from a similar fate. In 1987, the director of the National Archaeological Museum received a call in the middle of the night. Tomb-robbers had found the grave of a high-ranking Mochican warrior-priest and taken precious gold and silver treasure. Within hours, it would be headed for the black market – and out of the country. When he first arrived on the scene, the impoverished local community had descended upon the Huaca Rajada, consisting of two adobe pyramids and a low platform, in the hopes of finding valuable leftovers. With the help of the police, government funds and *National Geographic*, Alva and his team were able to persuade them to stop the looting. There, they uncovered the elaborate tomb of the Lord of Sipán, a Mochican lord, and six other people. A total of 451 ceremonial items were discovered at the site. Excavations continued, and two more tombs were found.

A World to be Discovered

Despite extensive efforts by archaeologists in Central and South America, the surface has only begun to be scratched. New cities remain to be discovered in the Honduran rainforest. Secrets remain hidden underneath the roads of Mexico City. And in the Andes, thousands of projects to uncover the legacy of the Inca and their predecessors continue. The challenges of looting remain. For archaeologists to be successful, academics and governments alike will have to remain vigilant against those who seek to plunder ancient tombs for wealth or fame.

THE COLLAPSE OF THE MAYA

Sophisticated civilization took longer to take root in the Maya lowlands than in the Mexican highlands. The environment was not a natural "cradle of civilization". Dense jungle, limited rainfall and dangerous wildlife made the establishment of empires in the region more difficult. Yet, by the middle of the 1st millennium CE, the Maya were the predominant power in Mesoamerica.

Excavations of the site of Cuello in northern Belize by Norman Hammond provide a fascinating insight into the emergence of this civilization. Maize husks discovered at the site have shown how the staple crop was responsible for an explosion of the Maya population. Both the size of the

THE MAYA ▼

1800 BCE–250 CE
Preclassic Maya
250–900
Classic Maya
500–600
The Rise of Tikal
750
Conflicts arise between Mayan city states and trading partners
750–900
Chichen Itza develops
899
Tikal is abandoned
900–1500
Postclassic Maya
900–1050
Chichen Itza becomes a regional power
1224
Chichen Itza is abandoned

maize cob and the yields of maize steadily increased between 1000 BCE and 200 CE. Hammond also discovered pieces of jade in graves, hinting that an élite was in place well before the Classic Maya period.

Great cities developed in the tropical jungles of the Yucatan. Beautiful sculpture, intricate artwork and spectacular pyramids displayed the influence of Mayan civilization for all to see. The Mayan command of mathematics and astronomy was extraordinarily advanced. Their hieroglyphic system of writing was as complex as it was intriguing. The exploration of Mayan civilization began with two Victorians, one American and one English: John Lloyd Stephens and Frederick Catherwood. Stephens was an explorer, writer and occasional politician, while Catherwood was an artist and engineer. They had both read intriguing accounts of lost cities hidden in the Mesoamerican jungle and set out to find them. In 1834, they arrived at Copan and soon moved on to chart the other great Mayan cities – Palenque, Uxmal and Chichen Itza. After returning to New York in June 1842, they jointly published *Incidents of Travel in Yucatán*, the following year. It was an illustrated account of the Mayan civilization that pioneered the study of the Maya as a serious archaeological subject.

JOHN LLOYD STEPHENS (1805–52)
FREDERICK CATHERWOOD (1799–1854)

John Lloyd Stephens and Frederick Catherwood recorded the ruins of Mayan civilization from Copan in the south to Chichen Itza in the north. Stephens' accounts of his travels in *Incidents of Travel in Central America, Chiapas and Yucatan* (1841) and *Incidents of Travel in Yucatan* (1843) with illustrations by Catherwood, brought the Maya civilization to international attention. When Catherwood published his book

Views of Ancient Monuments in Central America, Chiapas and Yucatan – a collection of lithographs (1844) it increased interest, pulling the Maya civilization out into a wider consciousness.

Stephens and Catherwood were not the first to explore the ancient Mayan sites, but they were the first to visit such a large number of sites and to record what they found accurately.

A portrait of John Lloyd Stephens from the frontispiece of his book, *Incidents of Travel in South America*.

Born in 1805 in Shrewsbury, New Jersey, John Lloyd Stephens graduated from Columbia University with a degree in law which he practised in New York until burdened by a throat infection, Stephens left New York on the advice of his doctor and travelled widely through Europe, the Mediterranean, the Middle East and North Africa. His first two books, *Incidents of Travel in Egypt, Arabia Petraea and the Holy Land* (1837) and *Incidents of Travel in Greece, Turkey, Russia and Poland* (1838) were based on these travels and proved very popular, and gave Stephens the sobriquet, 'the American Traveler'.

Frederick Catherwood was six years older than Stephens, an Englishman born in north London. Even by his twenties he had become well-known as an architect, artist and traveller, having already published his drawings of structures in Egypt, Palestine, Asia Minor and Greece. In 1833, he became the first Westerner to survey and draw the Dome of the Rock in

Jerusalem. In 1836, Stephens and Catherwood met in London where the latter's panorama of "The Ruins of Jerusalem" was on display. They discovered that they were both interested in exploring Mesoamerica and planned to travel together to the region at the first opportunity.

Stephens' renown as a traveller and writer was such that he was appointed US Ambassador to Central America by President van Buren. On 3 October 1839, he left New York with Catherwood for British Honduras (Belize). Although fully aware of his diplomatic duties, Stephens' main interest was to explore the ruin of Copan and then those at Palenque. By the mid-19th century, many Maya sites had become hidden from even the indigenous people of the region, their great temples and pyramids covered by vegetation and other accretions to become mounds and hills. Cities then known to exist included, Copan, Palenque, Topoxte/Tayasal and an unnamed city in the dense jungle that came to be known as Tikal. As there were no accurate maps of the region Stephens and Catherwood sometimes found sites through conversations with locals and other travellers; a key example of this was the discovery of Quirigua.

Unburdened by the great entourages which usually went with 19th-century explorations, they had just a guide, a few men to carry equipment, and a relatively basic and likely inaccurate map. Even with such a small and low-key staff, they explored the jungles of Mesoamerica to find the ancient sites of which they had read and heard tell. Stephens writes of his first impressions of Copan, reflecting that, "The sight of this unexpected monument put at rest at once and forever, in our minds, all uncertainty in regard to the character of American antiquities, and gave us the assurance that the objects we

were in search of were interesting, not only as the remains of
an unknown people, but as works of art, proving, like newly
discovered historical records, that the people who once
occupied the Continent of America were not savages."

With an offer of just $50, Stephens was able to buy the
city of Copan and was still considered a fool by the owner for
being prepared to buy such apparently useless land. His aim
was to try to move the whole city en masse to a museum in
New York. However, he did not find a way of doing so. His
time in the region convinced him that most existing theories
on the origins for the Maya ruins and their language were
entirely wrong and that the structures and language were
wholly indigenous.

Stephens and Catherwood explored each site together
and then took on their individual responsibilities for writing
about and drawing them up. Using a camera lucida that
projected the image onto paper to give an accurate outline,
Catherwood was able to draw impressions of the Mayan
sites that included the intricate scroll work and inscriptions
on the buildings. His drawings have been used to aid in the
restoration of the buildings and temples he drew. While he
may have used licence to compose his drawings for artistic
purposes, his depictions of the buildings are considered to
be completely accurate. Although he contracted malaria at
Palenque, Catherwood carried on working. It seems that
he refused to rest and did his drawings wearing gloves and
mosquito netting. Stephens, too, describes the many problems
encountered trying to get through to the remote sites,
including having to carve a route through the undergrowth as
well as the many stinging insects and potentially dangerous
animals that they encountered.

On their way to Uxmal, whose owner Stephens had met in New York and who had provided him with a map of the site, they discovered or documented Copan, Kabah, Merida, Palenque, Quirigua, Q'umarkaj (Utatlan), Sayil, Tonina, Topoxte, as well as Uxmal. They stayed at Uxmal, making extensive notes until the end of July 1840. By this time, Stephens had also contracted malaria and they returned to the US. The success of the book that resulted from these travels encouraged another trip to the Yucatan from 1841–42 which led to the publication of *Incidents of Travel in the Yucatan* and, later, Catherwood's book of lithographs, *Views of Ancient Monuments in Central America, Chiapas and Yucatan*. On this second trip they documented sites such as Ake, Chichen Itza, Dzibilnocac, Itzamal, Labna, Mayapan, Tulum, and went to Uxmal once more. In all they mapped, surveyed, drew and wrote about 44 distinct Maya sites, all of which have become national treasures and, some, world famous attractions.

After their second visit to Yucatan both men concentrated on other interests. Stephens ran the Ocean Steam Navigation Company and the Panama Railroad Company. It seems he was involved in an accident in either Panama or Bogota and died in New York in 1852 aged just 46. Catherwood went to California to open a supply store in San Francisco for miners who had flocked there after the 1849 Gold Rush. His reputation as an artist continued and his works were widely exhibited. Tragically, aged 55, he was among more than 350 passengers who died when SS *Arctic*, the ship he was travelling on, was rammed by the steam ship *Vesta* while in a fog bank.

Stephens' and Catherwood's meticulous work became the foundation of future studies of the Maya. Their writings and drawings were helpful to future travellers in uncovering more of the history; explorers such as **Desire de Charnay, Teobert Mahler, Alfred Percival Maudslay, Alfred Tozzer, Sylvanus Griswold Morley and Franz Bloom, all of whom made great strides in the understanding of this great, ancient civilization**

At the end of the 9th century CE, Mayan society collapsed with shocking suddenness. Inscriptions on monuments, tomb temples and royal funerary cults disappeared almost overnight. The great cities were abandoned and no new ones rose to replace them.

How did such a formidable civilization disappear so completely?

In the past, both historians and archaeologists pointed to factors such as civil war, invasion and the collapse of trade routes as the culprits. But today, most experts are looking to another explanation: man-made changes to the environment. Drought seems to have been a factor in the Mayan civilization's long decline. Population growth had spurred intense agricultural cultivation of maize in the region. This caused deforestation and the degradation of the soil, making the region simultaneously more vulnerable to flooding and drought. Far from being passive subjects of their environment, the Maya, like indigenous peoples across the Americas, had shaped the ecology they lived and worked within. In the 9th century, their impact on the environment caught up with them, and the record shows that the region suffered its worst drought for thousands of years.

The evidence has been growing. Douglas Kennett, heading a team of archaeologists, analysed thousands of samples of a 2,000-year-old stalagmite at Yok Balum cave in Belize to confirm the theory in 2012. In total, nine different institutions were involved in the project. Scientists from Rice University and Louisiana State University studied sediment samples from Belize's Great Blue Hole, a 400-ft (122-m)-deep cave in a barrier reef. Layers from the era of the Mayan decline between 800 and

1000 CE.showed the researchers the presence of high levels of aluminium and titanium that suggested that heavy rainfall from intense tropical cyclones was pounding material out of the rock and into the sea.

While the great cities of the south, such as Tikal and Palenque, were abandoned, in modern day Guatemala and Belize, the cities of the north continued to survive and even thrive, including the most famous of all Mayan cities, Chichen Itza.

An extended drought beginning in 1020 CE triggered political insecurity and increased warfare. This was followed by disastrous population collapse, perhaps the result of very sudden climate change. Even a minor drought could lead to the collapse of a carefully balanced ecosystem. By the time the Spanish conquistadors arrived in the 16th century, the great Mayan civilization was already fading into the jungle.

WILLIAM GADOURY

It took a tech-savvy, 15-year-old Canadian, William Gadoury, to locate a "missing" Mayan city hidden deep in the Yucatan peninsula. He proposed that the Mayan cities scattered through Mexico, Honduras, Guatemala and El Salvador lined up exactly with major stellar constellations. Yet one city appeared to be missing. He persuaded scientists at the Canadian Space Agency to focus its satellite imaging equipment on a significant spot where a star remained unmatched. Using Google Earth, he named the missing city K'aak Chi, or Mouth of Fire. Imagery of the site clearly showed a square, man-made formation concealed beneath the dense forest. The story attracted international attention, but some cast doubt on Gadoury's theory. Many archaeologists question if the Maya could have had the knowledge to arrange their cities in this highly symbolic way. Gadoury's extremely remote "lost" city remains as yet unexplored.

The
Archaeology
of Asia

From the Qin
to the Ming

The epic sweep of Chinese history between the coronation of the first Qin emperor, Qin Shi Huang (also known as Shi Huangdi), in 221 BCE and the fall of the Ming dynasty in 1644 CE saw a pattern of unification under an immensely powerful dynasty, followed by years of violent internal conflict.

A Unique Legacy

Archaeology has been practised in China since as long ago as the Song dynasty (960–1279 CE), when local gentry, scholars and bureaucrats recovered artefacts dating back to the Shang dynasty. Like the European antiquarians, their main interest was in acquiring ancient objects for their own personal pleasure rather than analysis of past cultures. Many hoped to use the artefacts they found for state rituals. The scholar Shen Kuo (1031–1095 CE) in his *Dream Pool Essays* castigated his contemporaries' superficial approach to archaeology and emphasized the importance of studying the original purpose and construction of ancient items.

Shen Kuo's warnings did not go entirely unheeded. Ouyang Xiu (1007–72 CE) created 400 rubbings of inscriptions found on bronze and stone relics, while Lü Dalin (1046–92 CE) made the practice of archaeology more systematic, creating the *Kaogutu*, or *Illustrated Catalogue of Examined Antiquity*, in 1092 which detailed the ancient objects that had been discovered. A formal system of dating soon followed, classifying objects according to their inscriptions, shapes and motifs.

Modern scientific Chinese archaeology began with the Swedish archaeologist Johan Gunnar Andersson (1874–1960). He arrived in China as a mining consultant. Working with Chinese colleagues such as Yuan Fuli, he found prehistoric remains in Henan Province along the Yellow River. In his role in China's National Geological Survey, he helped train a generation of Chinese archaeologists.

DYNASTIES OF CHINA

▼ **221 BCE–206 BCE**
Qin

206 BCE–220 CE
Han

220–280
Three Kingdoms

265–420
Jin

420–589
Northern and Southern dynasties

581–618
Sui

▼ **618–907**
Tang

907–960
Five Dynasties and Ten Kingdoms

960–1279
Song, Liao, Jin and Western Xia

1271–1368
Yuan

1368–1644
Ming

JOHAN GUNNAR ANDERSSON (1874–1960)

A Swedish archaeologist, palaeontologist and geologist, Andersson was influential in the development of archaeology in China in the 1920s. He studied first at Uppsala University and his initial research was in the polar regions, as director of Sweden's National Geological Survey.

He was on the Swedish Antarctic Expedition of 1901 to 1903, while his studies on the Falkland Islands and the Bjørnøya led him to come up with the term solifluction – a definition that was instrumental in the later definition of periglaciation.

In 1914 he went to China as a mining advisor as part of the National Geological Survey. He helped to train some of the first generation of geologists, as well as discovering many deposits of iron ore and other mining resources.

Andersson first went to Zhoukoudian, a cave system south-west of Beijing ,in 1918 to an area called "Chicken Bone

Hill" where rodent bones were found in large quantities. Returning three years later he was taken by local quarrymen to "Dragon Bone Hill" where he came across quartz that was not local to the area. Sensing that this could indicate the presence of early humans, he instructed his assistant Otto Zdansky to begin excavating the area in 1923 and much material was shipped to Uppsala for analysis. In 1926 Andersson announced he had found two human teeth, later identified as being the first finds of what became known as Peking Man.

With Chinese colleagues such as Yuan Fuli, Andersson found prehistoric Neolithic remains in 1921, at Yangshao in Henan Province, along the Yellow River. The prehistory of what is now China had not previously been investigated in scientifically organized archaeological excavations and the Yangshao and other prehistoric cultures had never before been recognized and investigated.

In the following years, 1923–24, Andersson, as part of China's National Geological Survey, ran archaeological excavations in Gansu and Qinghai provinces with Chinese colleagues, and published a number of books and papers on Chinese archaeology, many in the *Bulletin of the Museum of Far Eastern Antiquities*, which he founded in 1929, and published his most important scientific reports on his own work.

In 1926, Andersson set up the Museum of Far Eastern Antiquities in Stockholm, to house some of the items collected during the excavations in China. Although some of the Andersson collections were kept in Sweden, the rest, according to a bilateral Sino-Swedish agreement was returned to the Chinese government in seven shipments, from 1927–36. An exhibition of these objects was put on at the new National Geological Survey complex in Nanjing, where Andersson saw them in 1937.

The last documented evidence of the objects was a 1948 *Visitors' Guide to the Geological Survey* museum in Nanjing, which listed Andersson's Yangshao artefacts among the exhibits.

They were thought to have been lost forever in the civil war that followed. However, in 2002, following renovations at the Geological Museum of China, three crates of ceramic vessels and fragments were found and it was confirmed that these were indeed left from Andersson's excavations. Most of the items returned to China by Andersson are still sadly lost. This includes a spectacular and unique human-faced ceramic shaman head, and numerous fantastic painted ceramic vessels. Despite thorough investigations, their whereabouts remains unknown.

THE GREAT WALL OF CHINA

No single structure better encapsulates the reach, ambition and potency of China than the Great Wall. For the Chinese, it marked the point where civilization ended. A survey in 2012, using GPS and infrared to chart the course of the wall, concluded that its maximum length was a startling 13,247 miles (21,196 km). The emperor Qin Shi Huang began the construction of the "Long Wall of 10,000 Li" in the late 3rd century BCE to provide a defensive barrier against the nomadic Xiongnu people to the north. During the Han dynasty, it was needed to protect the increasingly vital trade routes of the Silk Road. By the 6th century, as many as 1.8 million men at a time were required to repair and reinforce the wall, and it would be repeatedly rebuilt over at least 1,700 years. It is hardly surprising, therefore, that many stretches of the wall remaining today, which are mostly the work of the Ming, look quite different from the original construction.

Honouring the Dead

Emperor Qin Shi Huang's achievements were astonishing – he united the warring kingdoms of China into a single empire, built the Great Wall and established China's legal and political system for years to come.

His final resting place was as magnificent as his reign. In 1974, farmers digging a well near the city of Xi'an stumbled across one of the greatest archaeological finds of Chinese history: the mausoleum of the first emperor. Among other surprises, the huge tomb complex revealed a pristine army of thousands of terracotta warriors guarding their emperor. The government dispatched a team of archaeologists to learn more. As many as 8,000 figures have been found in the tomb, along with horse-drawn chariots and weapons. Much of the subterranean complex remains unexcavated. Today, Chinese archaeologists using remote sensors have found another underground chamber, filled with figures posed as dancers, musicians and acrobats, but excavations have been temporarily halted for fear of damaging the site.

The most impressive of China's many other royal tombs – at least of those found so far – is at Mawangdui in Changsha in the centre of the country, where three 2nd-century BCE tombs were excavated between 1972 and 1974. When archaeologists opened up Tomb No. 1, that of Xin Zhui, the wife of the Marquis of Dai, they found it perfectly preserved. A wealth of artefacts were interred with her, including 152 "tomb figures" representing dancers, musicians and servants. There were everyday items, such as a tray with bowls and cups and a pair of chopsticks. Xin Zhui also took to her grave various cosmetic boxes, vases, arm rests and screens. On one side of the tomb were bamboo cases containing herbal medicines, silk garments and other clothes. Draped on the coffin was a spectacular T-shaped red silk banner representing her journey to the afterworld. Painted at the top is a vision of heaven, protected by two guards; below is an image of Xin Zhui flanked by two servants; and at the bottom are scenes from the underworld.

These impressive tombs required the work of thousands of labourers and provide compelling evidence of the wealth and reach of Han-dynasty China. Such marvellous burial procedures would not be seen again until the Ming dynasty.

Land of the Three Ways

By 500 BCE, Buddhism had spread rapidly across China. A series of sites discovered towards the end of the 19th century attest to the enduring vibrancy of the religion. At Dazu in Sichuan province, an exceptional series of religious figures were carved into the rock face.

Perhaps the single most remarkable site, however, is the warren of tunnels – the Caves of the Thousand Buddhas, or Mogao Caves – near the Silk Road settlement of Dunhuang in northwest China. They contain 487 lavishly decorated cave-temples, dug between 366 CE and 1368, and covering an area of 490,000 ft^2 (44,500 m^2). The first caves were discovered in 1900 by a Daoist monk, Wang Yuanlu. In the following years they were extensively investigated by teams from Britain, France, Japan and Russia.

In addition to 2,400 clay sculptures and 1,100 scrolls, 15,000 books printed on paper were found in what is known as the Library Cave. They were apparently hidden here for safe-keeping in approximately 1000 CE. Among the scrolls is a copy of the *Diamond Sutra*. Dating from 868 CE, it is the world's oldest complete printed document.

Maritime Traders

In recent times, archaeologists all over the world have increasingly used new technology to delve beneath the waves. China is no exception. In 1987, the Underwater Archaeology Research Centre was set up as a division of the National Museum of China. Its researchers have made impressive discoveries that are rewriting the history of China's maritime and trading past. Archaeologists are also unearthing evidence of an equally prosperous "Maritime Silk Road". In that same year, a team of British and Chinese archaeologists searching for an East India Company wreck instead found a 98-ft (30-m) 800-year-old Chinese shipwreck in the South China Sea. Nanhai No. 1 was dated to between 1127 and 1279 CE.

An extensive rescue operation began in 2007. Surveys of the wreck revealed that it contained more than 60,000 items. Following its transfer to the Maritime Silk Road Museum in Guangdong, excavation of the wreckage continued under the gaze of crowds of inquisitive tourists. The ship held porcelain and ceramics for trade, vast numbers of copper coins and personal items, including gold jewellery, which suggested that a number of wealthy merchants and passengers were on board when it sank. The vessel's importance as an archaeological find is rivalled only by the Terracotta Army.

All under Heaven

Modern China has spent billions creating a pool of well-trained state archaeologists, rebuilding its cultural identity after the Cultural Revolution. It is now even venturing outside its own borders, for example, with a dig in India at a Bronze Age site in Rakhigarhi, north of Delhi.

IMPERIAL FAREWELLS

If the Forbidden City in Beijing, begun in 1420, remains the most opulent expression of the lavish, highly ceremonial world of the Ming, the 13 Ming tombs, covering 15 miles^2 (40 km^2) at Changping, 26 miles (42 km) north of Beijing, are the dynasty's most compelling archaeological record. The remains of the Ming rulers from the Yongle emperor to the Chongzhen emperor lie in a series of mausoleums, the first constructed in 1409 and a final one completed on the death of the Ming emperor in 1644. Access to the tombs is via the "Sacred Way", an avenue lined with statues of lions, elephants, camels and bodyguards.

Only one of the 13 tombs has so far been excavated. This is Dingling, the tomb of Zhu Yijun (1572–1620), the terrifyingly corpulent Wanli emperor whose legendary indolence goes some way towards explaining the eventual collapse of Ming rule. It is the third-largest of the Ming tombs.

The frontispiece of the oldest known printed book in the world, a Chinese edition of the *Diamond Sutra*, found in the Mogao Caves in Dunhuang.

Built 89 ft (27 m) below ground, it had survived the centuries intact, safe from the depradations of looters and grave-robbers who have plagued so many archaeological sites. Following pleas from the archaeologists Guo Moruo and Wu Han in 1956, the site was hurriedly excavated on government orders. An astonishingly imposing complex, comprising five separate stone chambers behind two sets of immense self-locking marble doors, came to light. The fifth and final chamber was the tomb of the emperor and his two wives. Porcelain vases containing oil and a wick had been left to light the mausoleum for eternity.

The challenges faced by the Dingling excavation persuaded the Chinese government to suspend further excavation except for rescue purposes. The remaining Ming tombs are still unopened.

The Land of the Rising Sun

"The Ancestors" are very important in the spiritual life of Japan, and the Japanese have a long history of archaeological enquiry. The historian Lord Tokugawa Mitsukuni was eager to re-establish loyalty to the Japanese emperor. As early as 1692, he began Japan's first scientific excavation of an imperial tomb in Ohtawara City. It dated from the Kofun period (300–700 CE), Japan's early prehistoric era. These keyhole-shaped mounds (kofun) are unique to Japan.

The story of Japanese archaeology as a systematic discipline really began in 1877 when the American zoologist and orientalist Edward Sylvester Morse excavated the Omori Shell Mounds. Morse and his team discovered a style of pottery there that they described as "cord-marked". In Japanese, this translates as Jōmon, which became the term used for the early period of Japanese history (c. 14,000–1000 BCE), when this style of pottery was produced.

A fine example of Jōmon earthenware with its distinctive corded decoration and incised patterns.

Competing Theories

During the late 19th and early 20th centuries, Japanese scholars debated the origins of the Japanese people. Some believed they descended from a people called the Yayoi, who flourished from 300 BCE to 300 CE. Others believed the ancestors of the Japanese were the Ainu, the indigenous people of Hokkaido (Japan's second-largest island). Still others claimed the Japanese had the same ethnic origin as the Ryukyuan people, indigenous people of the Ryukyu Islands. An early aim of Japanese archaeologists was to test these theories. There were often racist undertones to these debates, as many scholars regarded the Ainu as "primitive", and were keen to disprove any ancestral connection between them and the "civilized" modern Japanese.

Western Techniques

In 1916, Japan's first university archaeology department was established at Kyoto Imperial University. The department's first professor, Kosaku Hamada, had spent time studying in Britain, and he introduced Western archaeological methods and theories to Japan on his return. In 1922, he published Japan's first ever archaeology textbook, *Tsuron Kokogaku* (*An Introduction to Archaeology*), which is still in print today. Hamada introduced the concept of seriation as a relative dating method for Japanese pottery. Seriation, developed by the Swedish archaeologist Oscar Montelius, looks at factors like design style and the quantity of objects sharing a particular style, as a way of establishing the chronology of an object. Through the use of this technique, Sugao Yamanouchi at the University of Tokyo was able to demonstrate that the Jōmon was a hunter-gatherer society, whereas the Yayoi was an agricultural one.

Using another Western technique, stratigraphy, Kosaku Hamada overturned myths about the prehistoric origins of the Japanese. In 1917, Hamada excavated at Kou, Osaka Prefecture, and in 1918–19, he excavated at Ibusuki, Kagoshima Prefecture. Here, the stratigraphy revealed that the Jōmon and Yayoi cultures came from different layers. Until this time, the two cultures were regarded as separate but contemporaneous. Hamada conclusively showed that the Jōmon culture pre-dated the Yayoi.

SHELL MOUNDS

Edward Morse's excavation at Omori, Japan, in 1877 was one of the world's first archaeological excavations of a shell mound. These are human-made mounds where the debris from cooking and eating shellfish have accumulated over time. They are useful to archaeologists as a record of people's diet, and also because they contain fragments of stone tools and household goods. Because shells are rich in calcium carbonate, shell mounds tend to be alkaline, which slows the normal rate of decay caused by soil acidity. This means that organic material, including food, clothing and human remains, often survives in shell mounds for archaeologists to study.

EDWARD MORSE (1838–1925)

Edward Morse was born in Portland, Maine, to a strict religious father and a mother who encouraged his interest in science. After being expelled from a number of schools for his unruly behaviour, Morse attended Gould Academy in Bethel, Maine where he met Dr Nathaniel True who encouraged him to pursue his interest in the study of nature.

In spite of his lack of formal education, the collections Morse put together during his adolescence took the interest of scientists from Boston, Washington and the UK. His work with land snails was notable, and he discovered two new species: *Helix milium* and *H. astericus* before he was 12.

After working as a mechanical draftsman and a wood engraver attached to a Boston company, Morse was recommended to Louis Agassiz at the Museum of Comparative Zoology at Harvard University for both his intellect and talent as a draughtsman. He was Agassiz' assistant in charge of the conservation, documentation and drawing collections of molluscs and brachiopods until 1861.

Unable through ill health to serve during the American Civil War, Morse married and had children and focused on his zoological work, specializing in the study of molluscs. In March 1863, he co-founded the journal *The American Naturalist*. He contributed to the journal and wrote two important books on molluscs which attracted the attention of Charles Darwin.

Morse first visited Japan in June 1877 to look for coastal brachiopods and stayed for three years when he was offered a post as the first Professor of Zoology at the Tokyo Imperial

University. While looking out of a window on a train between Yokohama and Tokyo, Morse discovered the Omori shell mound, the excavation of which opened the study in archaeology and anthropology in Japan, and shed much light on the material culture of prehistoric Japan. He returned to Japan in 1881 to present a report of his findings to Tokyo Imperial University.

A ceramics collector, antiquarian and sometime astronomer, Morse remained endlessly fascinated by a variety of subjects throughout his long life, continuing to travel widely and serve in a variety of institutions.

The Japanese Archaeological Association

The post-war period witnessed a major expansion of Japanese archaeology. The founding of the Japanese Archaeological Association (JAA) in 1948 led to an increase in collaboration among archaeologists from all over Japan.

The inspiration for the JAA was an excavation at Toro, an archaeological site in Suruga Ward, Shizuoka City, dated to the 1st century CE, which began in 1947. Discovered in 1943, Toro was the first archaeological site found to contain Yayoi-era wet-rice paddy fields. Also excavated at the site were pit-dwellings, refuse pits, raised-floor buildings and even the well-preserved remains of wooden farm tools. The excavation generated considerable interest from newspapers and radio stations, raising public awareness of Japan's ancient history.

The Toro excavation ended in 1950. Over the following eight years the JAA organized excavations at 21 other Yayoi-era sites, from Kyushu in the west to Aichi Prefecture in central Japan.

The JAA also played a major role in formulating rules governing archaeological excavations and the preservation of historic sites. This first became an issue following a fire that broke out in the great hall of Hōryūji, an ancient Buddhist temple in Nara, on 26 January 1949. Hōryūji dates from the 7th or 8th century and is one of the oldest wooden buildings in the world. The accident, which resulted in the destruction of several beautiful murals, prompted the Japanese national legislature to pass the Law of Protection of Cultural Properties (1950). The law, which the JAA helped to draft, codified the rules relating to archaeological excavations. Prior to 1950, anyone could excavate archaeological sites. From this point on, archaeologists had to obtain formal permission for an excavation from the national government.

Disaster-led Archaeology

Japan is one of the most earthquake-prone nations in the world, and this poses severe challenges for Japanese archaeology. Earthquakes can damage or destroy heritage and archaeological sites. In recent times, they have also become a galvanizing influence, spurring on archaeological excavations in the affected regions.

The Great East Japan Earthquake of 2011 devastated a vast area of the country, particularly Iwate, Miyagi and Fukushima Prefectures. The resulting tsunami reached more than 98½ ft (30 m) in height and swept several miles inland, destroying everything in its path. Almost 20,000 people were killed, and damage to the Fukushima No. 1 Nuclear Power Station led to serious radioactive contamination. In such tragic circumstances, damage to sites of cultural or historical interest may seem of minor concern. Yet damage there was, to more than 700 historic structures, including castles, fortresses, temples, shrines and other monuments. In Iwanuma City, the tsunami swept away ancient religious structures, and the Rikuzen-Takata municipal museum in Iwate was completely destroyed.

Another problem arose: Miyagi Prefecture has around 6,000 archaeological sites, and Iwate Prefecture has some 13,000, many of which have yet to be excavated. The majority of these sites are located in the hills above the devastated coastal plains – exactly where new homes were needed for those made homeless by the earthquake. So the authorities hastily recruited an archaeological labour force to excavate as many of these sites as possible before construction work began on the new towns. It was a race against time, but the teams worked quickly and efficiently.

In Iwate, a total of 557,743 ft^2 (51,816 m^2) was excavated prior to reconstruction at 30 sites. Many finds came to light as a result, altering understanding of local history. The archaeology teams held regular open days to share their discoveries with the public.

A similar emergency archaeology operation was carried out following the Great Hanshin Earthquake of 1995. Before the operation began, archaeologists were worried that they might be attacked by angry locals protesting at their presence in a disaster zone. To their surprise, the locals were fully supportive of the operation, and some 500 excavations were undertaken. The archaeologists who came out following the 2011 earthquake were similarly well received.

The archaeologists at Fukushima faced a more challenging situation, because many sites had suffered radioactive contamination. By donning hazmat suits, they were able to go out and rescue archaeological objects and store these for future display.

Despite the challenges, archaeology has transformed our understanding of the Japanese past. Many impressive remains have been unearthed in Nara, the capital of Japan between 710 and 784, including Buddhist temples, Shinto shrines and the Heijō Imperial Palace. In 1998, the palace and the surrounding area were made a UNESCO World Heritage site. A reconstruction of the palace now exists on the site and in 2010 a series of festivals and cultural events commemorated the 1,300th anniversary of the movement of the capital to Heijō-kyō (now called Nara).

THE POMPEII OF JAPAN

Kanai Higashiura in Gunma Prefecture has been dubbed the Pompeii of Japan. Like the Roman city of Pompeii, the site was buried and preserved under ash from an erupting volcano. In Japan's case, the volcano was Harunayama Futatsudake, and the eruption took place in the early 6th century CE, during the Kofun period. In the course of excavating the site in 2012, archaeologists discovered the well-preserved remains of a Japanese warrior wearing body armour. This kind of armour is known as kozaneko, and suggests a soldier of high rank. Many examples of kozaneko have been discovered over the years, but none until this one were worn by their owner. From his position, the soldier must have been brave, for he appeared to be on his knees facing the volcano when he was engulfed by the flood of molten rock and ash. Archaeologists have speculated that he may have been praying, trying to calm the volcano's wrath.

Learning from the Past

The 2011 earthquake inspired archaeologists, particularly in the Tohoku region, to go looking for traces of past earthquakes and tsunamis. They hoped that by uncovering evidence of these historic disasters, they might be able to help predict future ones. At Kutsukata, Sendai City, archaeologists found paddy fields dating from the middle Yayoi period, some 2,000 years ago. The fields were covered by a layer of white sand. By analysing the sand, they were able to determine that there had been a tsunami similar in scale to the 2011 one. In April 2014, the Nara National Research Institute for Cultural Properties began creating a database of historic natural disasters, recording the findings from Kutsukata and other places. A network of experts was set up to develop research methods and technologies for this new branch of geoarchaeology.

The Complexities
of the East

Much of Southeast Asia's rich archaeological legacy is under-explored compared with sites in Europe and the Americas, because governments in the region have devoted fewer resources to archaeological research. As a result, there may be many exciting discoveries still to be made, with the potential to shed new light on the region's history.

Supporting History?

Traditional histories of Vietnam tell of semi-legendary great kings nobly fighting for independence from their great northern neighbour, China. By contrast, early Chinese histories of the Vietnamese depict them as a savage people in need of civilizing. In the 1960s and 1970s, the Vietnamese government funded archaeological excavations seeking evidence to support the "great kings" theory of Vietnam's history. Excavations were carried out at

Co Loa, some 10 miles (16 km) north of Hanoi, on the Red River Delta. The delta is regarded by the Vietnamese as the birthplace of their civilization. The archaeologists were looking for evidence of a great civilization that might have flourished during the "middle phase" of Vietnamese history – after Neolithic times, but before the period of Chinese domination from 111 BCE.

What the archaeologists found did not support either the "great kings" or the "savages" version of Vietnamese history. They did not discover the ruins of splendid cities, but they did find walls built over a period of almost 60 years. A multigenerational project on this scale was most likely created by a complex society concerned with strengthening security and controlling its resources. The team also found tiles very similar to Chinese tiles long pre-dating the actual influx of their northern neighbours. This contradicted the traditional image of a fiercely independent people constantly at war with their powerful northern neighbour. Instead, it suggests that the Vietnamese traded and co-existed with the Chinese for much of their history.

Dating Controversy

Ban Chiang, in Nong Han District, Thailand, is perhaps the most famous Bronze Age site in all of Southeast Asia. It is also one of the most controversial. In August 1966, an anthropology student named Steve Young was living in Ban Chiang interviewing people for his senior honours thesis. While walking along a path, Young tripped over a tree root. On the ground, he saw the exposed top of a ceramic jar. After digging it out, Young noticed it had been fired using primitive techniques, but the design on the surface was unique and extraordinary. The following year, a systematic excavation of the site unearthed human skeletons, together with bronze grave

A truly amazing array of temples adorns the landscape at Bagan, the first capital of Myanmar.

goods and grains of rice. At first, archaeologists concluded it was a cemetery, but evidence of dwellings was later found, suggesting that the dead were buried next to or beneath their homes.

Archaeologists used thermoluminescence dating on the ceramic pots. This technique involves heating the ceramic and then measuring the amount of light it emits. This indicates the amount of electric charge that has built up within it and therefore its age. The result was quite a shock: the pots were dated to 4420–3400 BCE, making this the earliest Bronze Age culture in the world!

When a second excavation was carried out in 1974–75, sufficient organic material (rice and bone fragments) was collected from the site to carry out radiocarbon dating. The results suggested the site was more recent, with the oldest graves dating to about 2100 BCE, and the most recent to about 200 CE, while the earliest bronze objects were dated to 2000 BCE.

The new dates were not accepted by everyone, and it led to a heated debate about the site and its age. Over the years, evidence from subsequent excavations at this and other similar sites has given further support to the theory that Ban Chiang is a more recent settlement.

Temples in the Valley

The rich Buddhist and Hindu heritage of Southeast Asia is preserved in the many elaborate temples that dot the landscape. In Cambodia, the Angkor Wat complex is the largest religious monument in the world and attracts thousands of tourists each year. While pavements, roads and storerooms may have been reclaimed by the jungle, the temples continue to stand proud.

The medieval history of Myanmar, from around 600 to 1600 CE is the history of numerous peoples competing for the same territory along the fertile Irrawaddy River valley. They included the Mon, the Pyu, the Nan Chao, the Burmese, the Arakanese and the Shan. The most impressive legacies, however, were left by the Pyu, who dominated from 600 to 849, and the Burmese, who gained power from 849 to the late 1200s, centred on the city of Bagan, and who still dominate the country today. All of these cultures have been the focus of extensive archaeological excavations in Myanmar.

Tharay-khit-taya, situated 5 miles (8 km) from the modern town of Pyay in the north of the Irrawaddy, was the largest city of the Pyu. Intermittent archaeological work began here in 1907. Since 1964, archaeologists have worked intensively on the site, excavating and preserving monuments. Their efforts have revealed a circular city measuring 2.7 miles (4.4 km) in diameter, surrounded by a brick wall with 64 gates. The city contains stupas, pagodas, temples, residential buildings, a palace and 53 burial mounds. Archaeologists have found gold, bronze and stone statues, inscriptions in three languages, and urns inscribed with the names of kings and their dates.

Bagan was the capital of the first Burmese kingdom (known as Pagan). Most of its monuments were built between the 11th and 13th centuries when the kingdom was at its height. It rivals Angkor Wat in terms of its archaeological significance. More than 10,000 Buddhist temples, pagodas and monasteries were built in Bagan and its surrounding plains and the ruins of over 2,200 structures survive to this day. Ancient objects are preserved and displayed in the Bagan Archaeological Museum, established in 1902.

KAMBAWZATHADI ROYAL PALACE

The Kambawzathadi Royal Palace in Bago was built in 1556 by King Bayinnaung, founder of the second Burmese kingdom. The enormous palace contained 76 halls and apartments. The palace burned down in 1599, but excavation of the site was carried out in the 1990s, during which some 1,800 limestone sculptures of Buddha were unearthed. Based on knowledge gained from the excavations and original drawings of the building, part of the palace was reconstructed, including the Great Audience Hall and Bee Throne Hall.

Megalithic Monuments

Indonesia is rich in archaeological sites from every era of history. One of its most famous is the megalithic site of Gunung Padang in West Java, some 31 miles (50 km) southwest of the city of Cianjur.

Completed in about 5000 BCE, Gunang Padang is the largest megalithic site in all of Southeast Asia.

The complex consists of a terraced hill covering some 62 acres (25 hectares). Massive volcanic stones have been placed at the summit, which is surrounded by stone retaining walls that can be reached via 400 rock steps rising 311 ft (95 m). Locals regard Gunang Padang as sacred. According to folklore, it was built by King Siliwangi in a single night. It was not properly studied until 1979.

A 2012 survey revealed that its earliest parts date back 12,500 years. Artefacts found near the surface date to about 2800 BCE. Traces of 9,000-year-old glue have also been discovered, used to stick rocks together. Ground-penetrating radar revealed a large structure 49 ft (15 m) beneath the surface of the hill. According to geologist Dr Danny Hilman, the structure may contain chambers, terraces and rooms with steps. Hilman speculates that it could be a temple, built between 9,000 and 20,000 years ago. He has even suggested that the entire hill is an ancient pyramid. If true, this could indicate the existence of a hitherto unknown prehistoric civilization on Java with advanced engineering skills.

Others are more sceptical that such a civilization could exist, especially as there is no other evidence of its structures in the area. A set of primitive 9,000-year-old tools found in a nearby cave suggest that a simpler culture existed at this site.

Tombs and Temples

In the Bujang Valley in Malaysia, a sprawling complex of ancient ruins dates back more than 2,500 years. It covers an area of around 86.5 miles^2 (224 km^2), extending from Mount Jerai in the north to the Sungai River in the south. Archaeologists have unearthed more than 50 tomb-temples, called candi (pronounced "chandi"). Excavations have also revealed jetty remains, iron-smelting sites and a clay-brick monument. The Bujang Valley Archaeological Museum, located on the site, houses many of the artefacts discovered there, including inscribed stone tablets and caskets, metal tools, ceramics, pottery and Hindu icons.

During the 1950s and 1960s, research in the Bujang Valley was led by Western archaeologists including Horace Quaritch Wales, Dorothy Wales and Alistair Lamb. Since the 1970s, local archaeologists have continued the work there. With the support of the Malaysian government, they have carried out excavations and reconstructions. Since 2008, a team of Malaysian archaeologists have been excavating a port settlement in the Bujang Valley. In 2010, they unearthed a 1,900-year-old clay-brick monument built with geometric precision, possibly used for sun worship.

There have been setbacks: in December 2013, archaeologists at the site were outraged when a land developer demolished a 1,200-year-old Hindu temple (Candi No. 11). When challenged, the state government claimed the land was privately owned, so it was powerless to prevent it. In the wake of the controversy, Malaysia's Tourism and Heritage Ministry is considering declaring the Bujang Valley a heritage site, which will protect it from any future private development schemes.

The Riches of the Caves

The Manunggul cave complex in Lipuun Point, Palawan, in the Philippines was explored by a team led by Dr Robert Fox between 1962 and 1965. The team found human remains covered in red paint and wearing bracelets of jade, shells and stone beads. They also discovered an extraordinary burial jar, the Manunggul Jar. The lid featured a sculpture of a "spirit boat" carrying two souls to the afterlife. In 1965, Fox explored the Leta-Leta Cave in northern Palawan, a burial site dating to 1000–1500 BCE containing many stone and pottery artefacts. These included the famous "yawning jarlet of Leta-Leta", the earliest known pot in the Philippines.

In 2007, a team led by Dr Armand Mijares discovered a foot bone in Callao Cave near Peñablanca, Cagayan. The bone turned out to be 67,000 years old, making it the earliest known human fossil found in the entire Asia-Pacific region.

In Butuan City in 2012, archaeologists recovered the remains of an enormous boat called a balangay. The boat, estimated to be around 82 ft (25 m) long, could be up to 800 years old, long pre-dating the European ships that landed in the Philippines in the 16th century.

The earliest known document in the country is the Laguna Copper Plate, dated to around 900 CE. It was accidentally discovered in 1986 near the mouth of the Lumbang river. Written in Kavi, an old Javanese writing system, it turned out to be a receipt for the payment of a debt.

THE LIMESTONE TOMBS OF KAMHANTIK

Perhaps the most extraordinary of recent archaeological finds in the Philippines took place in 2011 on a jungle-covered mountain in Kamhantik. Here, archaeologists from the country's National Museum unearthed the remains of a village that could be up to 1,000 years old. At the site, they found 15 large limestone coffins dating to between the 10th and 14th centuries. The dating was based on an analysis of a human tooth found in one of the tombs. If it's correct, this would make them the earliest known limestone tombs in the

Philippines. Evidence from other sites of this era indicates that early Filipinos used wooden coffins. The limestone tombs were rectangular, resembling Egyptian sarcophagi, though simpler in design and with no ornamentation. Metal tools must have been used to carve them, indicating that the indigenous population was more technologically advanced than previously realized. Inside the tombs, the archaeologists found thousands of sherds of earthenware jars, metal objects and the bone fragments of humans, monkeys, wild pigs and other animals.

CITY OF TEMPLES

The modern state of Cambodia was dominated in the medieval period by the Khmer people. The greatest legacy of the Khmer is the Hindu temple complex of Angkor Wat, the largest religious monument in the world. Spread over a site of 403 acres (163 hectares), it is admired for its magnificent architecture and the beautiful carvings on its walls.

Angkor Wat is one of the most important archaeological sites in Southeast Asia, and the focus of ongoing study. In 1997, a team of archaeologists launched the Greater Angkor Project (GAP) to map the surrounding landscape, using ground surveys, aerial photographs and ground-penetrating radar. The project, completed in 2007, revealed that Angkor was far bigger than previously suspected. In fact, at its peak in the 12th century, it was the largest urban centre on Earth, with a population of around one million living in a network of suburbs.

The survey picked out 74 temple sites, more than 1,000 artificial ponds and a massive water system that linked the entire conurbation, supplying the Angkor residents with constant water, as well as irrigation for their crops. Angkor's success may have proved its undoing: the research

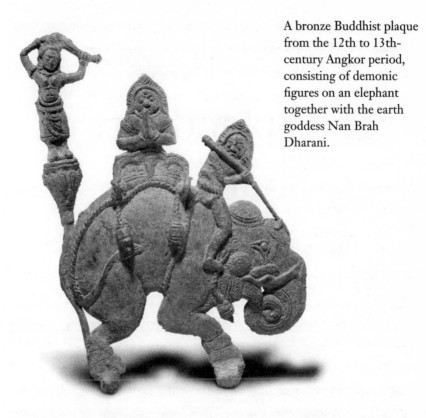

A bronze Buddhist plaque from the 12th to 13th-century Angkor period, consisting of demonic figures on an elephant together with the earth goddess Nan Brah Dharani.

showed evidence of overpopulation leading to deforestation and topsoil degradation that may have brought about Angkor's collapse.

Further studies of the site were carried out in 2012 and 2015 using cutting-edge airborne laser scanning (LiDAR) technology. By firing lasers at the ground from a helicopter, researchers were able to produce detailed imagery of sub-surface ruins. The laser scans identified earthen embankments built in geometric patterns, which may once have been gardens. They found evidence of towers that had been built and demolished during the construction of Angkor Wat, and a massive structure of unknown purpose to the south of the temple complex. The scans also revealed an area of low-density residential housing, with a road grid, ponds and mounds, possibly used by people working in the temple.

The Splendours of South Asia

As the location of one of the world's earliest civilizations, the Indus Valley, the history of South Asia (encompassing the present-day countries of Afghanistan, Bangladesh, Bhutan, India, the Maldives, Nepal and Sri Lanka) is a long one. The earliest known accounts of visitors to the area stretch back to that of Xuanzang, who came from China in the 7th century. Following him came others, such as Marco Polo, Ibn Battuta and Vasco da Gama.

A Western Obsession

Archaeological work in the area was first recorded in the 18th century. Sir William Jones founded the Asiatic Society in Calcutta in 1784 to promote the cause of Oriental research. Among the first Europeans to undertake excavations was Jean-Baptiste Ventura, an Italian mercenary hired to help modernize the Sikh army. He spent his spare time in Peshawar, excavating stupas in the Khyber Pass, in which he discovered Greek coins. In turn, he inspired the work of Alexander Cunningham, who in 1861 became the first surveyor general and director of the Archaeological Survey of India, which is responsible to this day for all archaeological work in India.

Alexander Cunningham became fascinated with Buddhist culture. As director of the Archaeological Survey of India, he led excavations at Sarnath and Bodh Gaya. He rediscovered Nalanda, a site that goes back to the time of the Buddha. There he excavated temples and palaces in two parallel rows, many of them with sculptural panels and elaborate walls of carved bead-and-reel decorations and wheel-and-deer insignia, along with plentiful evidence of early bronze casting.

Following in Cunningham's footsteps came the likes of Robert Bruce Foote and Sir John Marshall, with the latter adding extensively to the history of South Asian civilization with his meticulous excavations at Mohenjo-Daro and Harappa.

ALEXANDER CUNNINGHAM
(1814–93)

Cunningham was born in London, the son of Scottish poet
Allan Cunningham and his wife Jean. He and his brother
Joseph were educated at Christ's Hospital, London and gained
cadetships at the East India Company's Addiscomb Seminary,
followed by technical training at the Royal Engineers' Estate
at Chatham. Joining the Bengal Engineers at the age of 19 as
a second lieutenant, Alexander spent the next 28 years serving
the British government of India. There in 1833, he met James
Prinsep, an English scholar, orientalist and antiquarian and
over the next few years became his friend, confidant and pupil.
This friendship led Cunningham to his abiding interest in
Indian archaeology and antiquity.

From 1836 to 1840 he acted as ADC (aide-de-camp) to
Lord Auckland, the governor-general of India during which
time he visited Kashmir, a little-explored part of the country.
From 1841–46 he served in a number of positions and places
and saw action several times. In 1846 he was appointed
commissioner with P. A. Vans Agnew to demarcate India's
boundaries. Lord Hardinge wrote letters to Chinese and
Tibetan officials but there was little response. Cunningham
led a second commission in 1847 to establish the Ladakh–
Tibet boundary. The commission was set up to delimit the
northern boundaries of the empire after the First Anglo-Sikh
War concluded with the Treaty of Amritsar, ceding Kashmir
to Britain.

Cunningham's Essay on the *Aryan Order of Architecture*
(1848) was informed by his visits to temples in Kashmir and

his travels in Ladakh. At the same time, he was at the battles of Chillianwala and Gujrat. In 1851, with Lieutenant Maisey, he explored the Buddhist monuments of Central India, writing an account of their travels later.

From 1856 he served as chief engineer of Burma and from 1858 as chief engineer in the North-Western Provinces, establishing public works departments in both regions. He was not in India during the Rebellion of 1857. Appointed colonel of the Royal Engineers in 1860, he retired on 30 June 1861, in the rank of major general.

Cunningham had taken a keen interest in antiquities from early in his career, providing an appendix to James Prinsep's article on the relics in the Mankiala stupa in the *Journal of the Asiatic Society of Bengal*. He undertook excavations at Sarnath in 1837, making careful records in words and drawings of the sculptures. He dug at Sankassa in 1842 and at Sanchi in 1851. *The Bhilsa Topes* published in 1854 was an attempt to link the history of Buddhism to available architectural evidence. At the same time, he was writing to William Henry Sykes and the East India Company about the importance of an archaeological survey. His rationale was to show how India had been stronger as a single entity than as numerous small chiefdoms, and also that Hinduism was not ancient and immutable, but of comparatively modern origin and constantly subject to alteration – something he argued would prove that it was important for Christianity in India to ultimately succeed.

After his retirement from the Royal Engineers in 1861, Earl Canning, the viceroy of India, appointed Cunningham archaeological surveyor to the government of India, an appointment he held from 1861–65, when it was terminated through lack of funds.

Alexander Cunningham (fourth from right), the first director of the
Archaeological Survey of India.

When trying to identify cities mentioned in ancient Indian
texts many antiquarians used clues found in classical Graeco-
Roman chronicles and in the accounts of travellers to India
such as the Chinese Xuanzang and Faxian. Cunningham
recognized a number of cities mentioned by Xuanzang
and also identified cities including Ahichchhatra, Bairat,
Kaushambi, Nalanda, Padmavati, Sangala, Sankisa, Shravasti,
Srughna, Taxila, and Vaishali. To confirm his identifications,
he also used field surveys. The identification of Taxila was

tricky because of errors in the distances given by Pliny in his *Naturalis Historia* which suggested a location on the Haro river, two days' march from the Indus. Cunningham saw that this location did not tally with that given in the itineraries of Chinese pilgrims, most notably, the descriptions of Xuanzang. The Chinese sources recorded that the journey to Taxila from the Indus took three days, not two suggesting a different location for the city. His subsequent explorations in 1863–64 of a site at Shah-dheri convinced him that he was correct.

When his department was terminated, Cunningham returned to England to write the first volume of his *Ancient Geography of India* (1871), which covered the Buddhist period; but he failed to complete the second volume on Muslim rule in India. He also worked as director of the Delhi and London Bank. When in 1870 Lord Mayore set up the Archaeological Survey of India, Cunningham returned to India as its director-general at the start of 1871, making field explorations each winter and carrying out excavations and surveys from Taxila to Gaur. He made 24 reports, 13 as author with the rest under his supervision. His other works in this time included the first volume of *Corpus inscriptionum Indicarum* (1877) which included copies of the edicts of Ashoka, the *Stupa of Bharhut* (1879) and the *Book of Indian Eras* (1883). He retired from the Archaeological Survey in 1885 at the age of 71, and returned to London to continue his research and writing. Cunningham also amassed extensive collections of artefacts. Although some of his treasures were lost, most of the gold and silver coins and an excellent group of Buddhist sculptures and jewellery were purchased in 1894 by the British Museum.

THE *RIG VEDA*

The *Rig Veda* consists of 1,028 hymns dedicated to the
multitude of deities of the Aryan peoples who appeared in
India for the first time in about 1500 BCE. It can scarcely be
regarded as an historical record: not only is there no attempt
at any kind of history telling, but it is also widely assumed to
have been written down several hundred years after the period
it refers to. Its importance, however, is that it was written in
Sanskrit, the language of the Aryans and the distant ancestor
of Greek and Latin. Veda, for example, is simply the Sanskrit
word for "knowledge".

Many Empires

After the disappearance of the Indus Valley civilizations came what
has been called the Indian Dark Age, which began at some point
around 1500 BCE. A written record of sorts exists of these turbulent
centuries. This is the Hindu *Rig Veda*, the oldest religious text in the
world, composed between 1700 and 1100 BCE. In every important
respect, it marks the birth of Hinduism, and the India that emerged
in the confused and hazy aftermath of the Indus Valley civilizations.

It was a period that saw the rise and fall of a series of north Indian
empires and the settlement of much of the south of India, particularly
around Chennai, Mysuru and Kerala. Here, however, hilly and
often impenetrable jungle militated against the development of
larger political entities. Critically, however, even in the north where
central control was strongest, India was increasingly marked by a
religious diversity that continues to this day.

The major theme that emerges from the first part of this period is the appearance of the Aryans and their gradual eastward settlement of the river valleys of the Yamuna and, especially, the Ganges, both flowing into the Bay of Bengal. This eastward movement is amply attested by finds of pottery known as Painted Grey Ware. Two sites stand out: Mathura, claimed as the birthplace of the Hindu god Krishna; and Ahichatra, the latter inhabited continuously from 600 BCE to 1100 CE and first excavated from 1940 to 1944.

In addition to the Aryans' development of an extraordinarily complicated metaphysical belief system, what most obviously characterized the early centuries of Aryan settlement was their protracted struggle with the native Dasas. The latter's eventual defeat was possibly the origin of the Hindu caste system as the Dasas became the untouchables.

The settlement of the Ganges was evidently well under way before 1000 BCE. It was critically dependent on the growth of rice, which became the staple crop of the region. Nonetheless, by 500 BCE, a more-or-less well-defined series of 16 states or "mahajanapadas" had emerged across the Gangetic plains. Their numbers were then gradually reduced to four, of which Magadha, with a substantial capital on the banks of the Ganges, Pataliputra, would emerge at the end of the 4th century BCE as the core of the first great Indian empire, the Mauryan. Hardly less important, it was here that both Buddhism and Jainism were developed.

The Mauryan empire was the creation of a prince, Chandragupta. In c. 325 BCE he staged a coup, seizing the throne of Magadha and then extending its rule well to the east and the south. Pataliputra remains the most obvious expression of this first phase of Mauryan rule. Though much lies underneath today's city of Patna, what has been excavated reveals a city of astonishing size and sumptuousness.

Mauryan India reached its peak under the rule of Chandragupta's grandson, Asoka, in the 3rd century BCE. As his empire grew, so Pataliputra grew, too. It was claimed to have held a population in excess of 150,000 and its wooden walls had "570 towers and 64 gates". No less important, its architecture, especially the monument called the "Pataliputra capital", betrays clear Persian and Greek influences, the result of Alexander the Great's conquests first of Persia, then of India, where he reached the Indus in 327 BCE. It presaged a cultural exchange between the Middle East and northern India that would endure for centuries.

At least as lasting an influence from Asoka was his championing of Buddhism. It was made possible by an exceptionally well-organized administrative system, one set out in a work known as the *Arthashastra*, written by Chandragupta's chief minister, Kautilya. It resulted in the building of an estimated 84,000 stupa, hemispherical monuments built either of stone or brick and generally containing relics, sometimes burials. The most celebrated is that at Sanchi, built and rebuilt between the 3rd century BCE and the 12th century CE. No less characteristic was the construction of a series of imposing stone pillars, similarly proclaiming Buddhist teachings, many topped by lions and/or a wheel, symbolizing the world. Asoka himself was hailed as a chakravartin, or "wheel turner".

The Mauryan empire was short-lived. It was followed by a confused series of invasions and settlements, of territorial seizures and sudden collapses. The most enduring of these settlements was the Kushana empire that in the 300 years up to approximately 300 CE laid claim to most of northwest India. The rise of the Roman empire at least re-established the subcontinent's trading links to the wider world. By the 1st century CE, Pliny in Rome was bemoaning the excessive cost of imported luxury Indian goods. In turn, the Mediterranean shipped wines, copper, dates, slaves and pearls to India. Overland trade with China similarly burgeoned.

A further empire followed, that of the Guptas, who from about 300 CE took over and extended Pataliputra, from where they ruled an empire that almost rivalled the Mauryan in extent. Their energetic promotion of Hinduism has led many to call Gupta India the Classical Age of India. In fact, Gupta rule never extended to the southern tip of the sub-continent, where prosperity was markedly increased both in and around Madras and in Sri Lanka, and it was brought to a sudden and violent end in about 480 CE.

Nomadic warrior invaders from central Asia, the White Huns, descended on India. India was reduced to "a patchwork of petty kingdoms squabbling among themselves". It would take until the 16th century for India to re-emerge on the world stage.

Holy Men and Sages

As early as 327 BCE, when Alexander the Great reached the borders of India on his epic campaigns, India's reputation in the ancient world as a land celebrated for its holy men and sages was already established.

Buddhism spread astonishingly rapidly across much of East and Southeast Asia. Mahayana Buddhism placed great importance on images of the Buddha himself. The creation of such images was considered a worthy deed in itself. Thus, from the 1st century CE, it led to a proliferation of carved images of the Buddha and those semi-divine beings, the Bodhisattvas, across central India.

Of the multitude of surviving examples, the oldest was discovered in 2013 at Lumbini in Nepal, traditionally claimed as the birthplace of Siddhartha Gautama, the Buddha himself. The excavations were undertaken by a team led by British archaeologist Robin Coningham. If its provisional date of 550 BCE is correct, it would mean that 563 BCE, the date traditionally said to mark the birth of Siddhartha Gautama, might be too late by perhaps a century, as ritual practices of Buddhism were already well underway.

The vast majority of such images were produced only from the 1st century BCE. There were two main centres: Gandhara, an area that straddles northwest India as well as parts of Pakistan and Afghanistan; and the northern Indian city of Mathura. The Gandhara statues show clear influences of Greek statuary. The finest example, dating from the 2nd or 3rd centuries BCE, is held in the British Museum in London. It comes from a Buddhist monastery at Jamal Garhi, close to the town of Mardan in Pakistan. The monastery was discovered in 1848 by Alexander Cunningham. It was ten years later that the statue itself, along with many others, was discovered during an archaeological expedition led by another British army officer, Lieutenant Cromten.

THE SANCHI MONASTERY

The enduring significance of Asoka's embrace of Buddhism found expression in his creation of a series of monasteries. Of them, that at Sanchi in central India, rebuilt in the 1st century CE, remains the most commanding. It is in the form of a stupa, a symbolic structure, a hemispherical dome, raised over holy relics and acting as "an architectural diagram of the cosmos", with the dome a representation of the heavens. Circling it is an immense stone fence, pierced by four gates, each aligned to the four cardinal points of the compass. It was only in 1912, when the site was taken over by the Archaeological Survey of India, that the first serious attempts at its preservation were made.

Heritage at Risk

At Bamiyan in central Afghanistan, two Buddhas were carved in the 6th century CE into a cliff face, one 115 ft (35 m) high, the other 174 ft (53 m) high. In 2001, both were destroyed by the Taliban. The resulting international outrage led to a sustained archaeological effort that in 2004 revealed the existence of 50 hitherto unknown caves, in 12 of which wall paintings of Buddhas were discovered. Painted with an oil-based mixture, they have been confirmed as the oldest-known oil paintings in the world.

A no less remarkable example of the vivid tradition of Buddhist visual art is provided by the Ajanta caves in Maharashtra in western

An intricate statue of the Buddha lies in the centre of the Ajanta caves in western India.

India. In Western terms, they were discovered in 1819 by yet another British army officer, John Smith. The work of creating the caves was concentrated into a relatively brief period between 460 and 480 BCE.

These and other examples of early craftsmanship were the precursors of the artistic work created in the centuries that followed, including that of the Mughal empire, renowned for its artwork.

Developments
in Archaeology

The Holy Land

The Bible is both a sacred text and an extraordinary historical document, containing a wealth of information about the Holy Land in ancient times. These two perspectives have driven the field of biblical archaeology. More than 150 years ago, the first biblical archaeologists went out, a Bible in one hand and a trowel in the other, attempting to confirm the truth of holy scripture. Interest has moved away from literal authentication of the Bible and focuses on illuminating the background to the Judaeo-Christian tradition.

Biblical archaeologists disagree on the scope of their research. Some biblical archaeologists examine the period from c.8000 BCE to 600 CE, the date of the earliest remains of Jerusalem up to the invasions by the Islamic armies, while others study a narrower period, from 2000 BCE, the time of the Hebrew patriarch Abraham, to 100 CE, the death of John the Evangelist. Similarly, the Holy Land itself is an imprecise term. Its core is the southern Levant, including modern Israel, Palestine and Jordan, but many think it should include peripheral lands mentioned in the Bible, such as Egypt, Syria and Mesopotamia.

The Good Book and a Compass

The origins of modern biblical archaeology can be traced to the mid-19th century when European archaeologists such as Edward Robinson, armed only with compasses and Bibles for reference, ventured into the Holy Land. In 1867, Charles Warren and Charles William Wilson investigated the Temple in Jerusalem, and in 1870 French archaeologist Charles Clermont-Ganneau studied the inscriptions on the Mesha Stele in Jordan. The British, French, American and German governments all, at various times, funded archaeological expeditions to the Holy Land, with the sole objective of proving that the biblical stories were true.

The period of British Mandate Palestine (1922–48) witnessed a dramatic expansion in biblical archaeology. By this time, the field had split into two broad schools of thought: the "minimalists", who believed the Bible to be a non-historical, religious document, and the "maximalists", who held that it should be accepted as history unless archaeology proved otherwise.

The dominant figure working at this time was American scholar William Albright. Albright strongly believed that archaeology proved the truth of the biblical narrative. The British archaeologist Kathleen Kenyon, who led excavations at Jericho and the Ophel of Jerusalem, challenged this view in the 1950s.

She and others found evidence that demonstrated clear discrepancies between the Bible stories and the facts on the ground. After the establishment of the state of Israel in 1948, Israeli archaeologists entered the field. Following Israel's victory in the 1967 Six-Day War, they expanded their activities into Jerusalem and the occupied West Bank. Benjamin Mazar, for example, excavated parts of Jerusalem's Temple Mount.

THE DEAD SEA SCROLLS

Biblical archaeology's most important find came in 1947 when a Bedouin shepherd boy, Muhammad Edh-Dhib, searching for a lost goat in the Judaean desert, entered a cave where he found some ancient jars. The jars, he discovered, contained scrolls. His find would later be dubbed the Dead Sea Scrolls. Subsequent excavations yielded some 800 of these scrolls in tens of thousands of fragments, dating from between 300 BCE and 100 CE. Written in Hebrew, Aramaic and Greek, they

contained biblical works, as well as prayers and legal texts. This makes them by far the earliest versions of any part of the Bible ever found.

The Israelites

Most biblical archaeologists practising today would agree that the Bible stories about the early Israelites – Abraham, Isaac, Jacob, Joseph, Moses, Joshua, etc – were really stories deriving from historical memories. There is no archaeological evidence to suggest the Israelites were in Egypt, or that they wandered the desert, or conquered Canaan in a military campaign. The kingdom of David, portrayed in the Bible as a major regional power, was probably a small tribal chiefdom.

The Merneptah Stele, discovered by the Egyptologist Flinders Petrie in 1896 at Thebes, dated to 1206 BCE, mentions a list of peoples and city-states in Canaan. Among them is Israel, described as a people rather than a state. Excavations in the 1970s by Israeli archaeologists surveyed the lands of former Canaan – the central highlands north and south of Jerusalem, and lower Galilee – and found the remains of small, hilltop villages dating from the 13th and 12th centuries BCE. Today, more than 300 of these villages have been found.

Contrary to Biblical stories of military conquest by invading Israelites, the archaeologists found no evidence of armed conflict. They appear to have been settled peacefully over a prolonged period. Many scholars now think the Israelites were in fact Canaanites who settled in this region after being displaced from the lowlands and river valleys.

Archaeologists have found evidence of an Israelite kingdom in the 9th and 10th centuries BCE. An inscription found at Tel Dan in northern Israel, dated to 840 BCE, mentions a "House of David". There is also evidence to support the biblical assertion that King Solomon strengthened the defences of three of his cities, Hazor, Megiddo and Gezer. Between 1957 and 1970, Israeli archaeologist Yigael Yadin worked at these sites and discovered that the gates in each city were of identical construction and design, which seems to support the Bible's account.

One God or Two?

According to the Bible, the Israelites embraced monotheism from the time of Moses. The élites may have done so, but did ordinary Israelites? In 1968, American archaeologist William Dever came across a Hebrew inscription in an 8th-century BCE cemetery at Khirbet el-Qîm, near Hebron. It referred to "Yahweh and his Asherah". Asherah is the name of a Canaanite mother goddess. Ordinary Israelites may still have worshipped one of the old goddesses alongside the Israelite god Yahweh, centuries after Moses. In the 1970s, many more inscriptions were found linking Yahweh with Asherah. Moreover, in tombs and dwellings throughout the region, figurines have been unearthed of a female deity dating from the 6th to 10th century. In Dever's view, Judaism did not become fully monotheistic until the Babylonian Exile in the 6th century BCE.

WAR OF THE WALLS

Did Joshua burn the walls of Jericho? One of the most controversial arguments in biblical archaeology was on this point. During excavations there in the 1930s, led by John Garstang, a stratum of burnt material was found at a level

known as City IV, indicating that the city had been destroyed
by fire. Garstang dated City IV to 1400 BCE, corresponding
to the time in the Bible when the Israelites, under Joshua,
destroyed the city. However, when Kathleen Kenyon studied
the site in the 1950s, she redated the destruction layer to
1550 BCE. Using today's more precise radiocarbon dating,
Dutch archaeologists Hendrik Bruins and Johannes van der
Plicht now place the burned stratum at 1562 BCE, confirming
Kenyon's thesis. Although the biblical story may not be
correct on all specifics, Kenyon was able to delineate more
than 20 distinct time periods in the city, observing three major
destructions. She also found evidence of a siege, including
grain being burned to stop besiegers taking the city and
profiting from the supplies.

Bringing the Scriptures to Life

When a biblical archaeologist makes a find, it is likely to generate
headlines. One only has to look at the many claims people have
made to have found the Ark of the Covenant. Today, biblical
archaeologists are more rigorously scientific in their methods than
the early pioneers, and they are no longer intent on trying to prove
the veracity of Bible stories. Instead, they are driven by a desire to
discover the material remains of the Bible lands and shine a light on
a long-vanished world.

Going into Battle

History, as is often said, is written by the victors. Until recently, those who tell the stories of past battles have tended to rely on written sources, which can be unreliable or biased. It is difficult to disentangle the truth from the mayhem that happens on the battlefield, but archaeology is a formidable weapon....

Since the 1980s, historians have deployed a powerful new weapon to understand the reality: archaeology. It answers the questions: how did the battle unfold? What were the experiences of ordinary soldiers? And what factors influenced the outcome?

A New Field of Study

Battlefield archaeology was "invented" in 1984, when American archaeologist Douglas Scott set out to investigate the site of the 1876 Battle of Little Bighorn, in Montana, USA. In the course of battle, the US Army's 7th Cavalry, led by George Custer, was wiped out by Sioux and Cheyenne forces. Armed with metal detectors, Scott and his team researched the battlefield as if it were a crime scene. By locating and analysing bullets and cartridges in various parts of the site, they attempted to show exactly where the US forces were in relation to the Native Americans, where confrontations and skirmishes took place and how the troops moved around the battlefield. By these means, Scott constructed a precise timeline of the battle.

Some experts disputed Scott's analysis because the topography of the site had altered since 1876. Furthermore, over the years, relic hunters had stolen a considerable number of cartridges and bullets. Battlefield archaeologists have often faced this type of criticism, and with some validity. Historical documents provide necessary context for the evidence found in the ground.

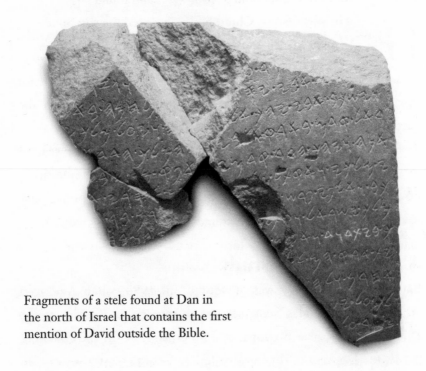

Fragments of a stele found at Dan in the north of Israel that contains the first mention of David outside the Bible.

THE BATTLE OF TEUTOBURG FOREST

In 1988, Major Tony Clunn, a hobby archaeologist stationed in Germany with the British army, armed himself with a metal detector and began searching for the site of the famous Battle of the Teutoburg Forest (9 CE) in which three Roman legions had been wiped out in just four days. After surveying the Kalkriese area – identified with the help of a local archaeologist, Dr Schluter, and various military accounts – Clunn recognized the distinct relationship between the hills to the south, known as the Kalkriese Berg, the moor and the military road to the north. He mapped out a survey grid and worked his way methodically across it. There, he detected pieces from three lead Roman slingshots and found large numbers of silver coins. Clunn had discovered the site of one of the Western world's most important battlefields. Kalkriese was a bottleneck, and as a military man, Clunn correctly identified the area where the Roman army had been caught between a hill and a moor.

Tools and Methods

The metal detector is one of the most important tools used by the battlefield archaeologist, to locate metal artefacts – weapons and ammunition – dropped during the fighting.

But battlefield archaeology also requires teams of specialists. Topographical scientists create detailed contour maps of the battlefield. Geophysicists use ground-penetrating sensors to analyse subsurface features. Excavators open up sections of ground, making notes and taking photographs as they dig deeper. Conservators detail the recovered artefacts. Anthropologists study human remains. Experts in historical weapons analyse recovered weapons and ammunition. Gradually, they build up a detailed picture of the battle.

THE BATTLE OF CULLODEN

Metal detectors proved extremely useful to archaeologists studying the Battle of Culloden, the climactic confrontation of the Jacobite Rising. On 16 April 1746, the Jacobite forces of Charles Edward Stuart (Bonny Prince Charlie) were crushed by loyalist troops led by William Augustus, Duke of Cumberland. The last pitched battle fought on British soil took place on a rain-blasted moor outside Inverness in Scotland. More than 250 years later, in 2005, a team of archaeologists was able to establish the exact location of the left flank of the Hanoverian (British) line, and where it was struck by the charging Jacobite cavalry. They were also able to show that the battlefield covered a much wider area than was previously thought.

The Battle of Bosworth Field

The battle at Bosworth Field in Leicestershire on 22 August 1485 changed the course of English history. Richard III, the reigning Yorkist king and last of the Plantagenet line, was killed. The victor that day, Henry Tudor, was crowned King Henry VII on the field. The Tudor dynasty ruled from then on, until 1603. Yet for all its significance, the location of the battle remained in question.

For more than 200 years, the site of the clash was generally accepted to be Ambion Hill, near Sutton Cheney, Leicestershire. A stone memorial marks the spot where Richard III supposedly died. In 2004, Leicestershire County Council asked battlefield archaeologist Dr Glenn Foard to investigate the truth of this claim. Foard assembled a multidisciplinary team to search for the core site.

First, they reviewed the original documentary evidence. Written sources confirmed the presence of a contemporary marsh. The team carried out an exhaustive survey of a 2.7 mile^2 (7 km^2) area that encompassed all reasonable candidates for the marsh. Analysing early names for local fields, furlongs and other sites, they mapped the soils and peat deposits to establish where a marsh might have dried up.

This reconstruction of the medieval landscape led them to a promising candidate. Pollen analysis, followed by Carbon-14 dating of peat deposits, revealed an area that would have been a marsh at the time of the battle.

A silver-gilt badge depicting a boar that was found at the new site of the Battle of Bosworth.

They carried out a systematic archaeological survey with metal detectors. They sweep-detected 22 lead artillery round shot and bullets fired from early handguns. The largest calibre, 93 mm shot, tells us that the gunners at Bosworth Field were already deploying the lethal medium-sized cannon known as a saker.

In the end, an extraordinary chance find finally pinned down the battlefield's exact location: a silver-gilt badge in the form of a boar – the personal emblem of Richard III. Here was conclusive proof. Four years of hard, intensive archaeological investigation had paid off. The "new" Bosworth Field straddles the Fenn Lane Roman road, near Fenn Lane Farm. It is some 1.8 miles (3 km) to the southwest of Ambion Hill.

DISCOVERING RICHARD III

In 2012, when a skeleton was found underneath a Leicester car park with a very pronounced curve in the spine, even osteologists were convinced they had finally found Richard III. There was evidence of scoliosis in many of the vertebrae. These bones should be symmetrical, but were not. Richard's right shoulder was noticeably higher than his left. The disease would have got worse as he got older, put pressure on his lungs, and may have caused shortness of breath. In the case of Richard III, the evidence was overwhelming, and subsequently confirmed by DNA analysis. The remains of the king were finally laid to rest in Leicester Cathedral on 26 March 2015.

Finding a Site

It is striking how a single battle can transform the language, culture and subsequent history of an entire country, or even, as in the case of Kalkriese and Alesia, alter the destiny of a major part of the European continent.

When in 52 BCE, a Roman invasion force under Gaius Julius Caesar defeated a formidable alliance of Gaulish tribes led by Vercingetorix at the hilltop oppidum of Alesia in France, it was no small victory. Roman rule, law and customs gradually took over.

Southeast of Montbard, in modern-day Burgundy, what is now at stake is not a culture, but expert reputations. The modern archaeological battle centres on whether or not the Gaulish oppidum, or Celtic hilltop fort near the modern village of Alise-Sainte-Reine, really is where this battle took place.

Napoléon III had a giant statue of Vercingetorix erected at Alise-Sainte-Reine in 1865, and, in 2012, a visitors' centre was built close by, at a cost of some €75 million. Huge investment has gone into this site. But there is a problem: a key site – Chaux-des-Crotenay, in the Jura mountains some 35 miles (56 km) from Geneva – continues to challenge the official view.

Both sides in the dispute cite archaeology as the decisive authentication. At the Chaux site, archaeologist André Berthier found the remains of a 33-ft (10-m)-high Bronze Age rampart, and a rare stone watchkeeper "goddess", along with various Celtic artefacts and the possible remains of a Roman military encampment.

Alise-Sainte-Reine's backers cite the major excavations carried out in the 1860s, which unearthed Celtic and Roman artefacts. But the "Jurassics", as their opponents call them, believe these may have been planted by Napoléon III's workers. Against this, a Franco-German dig in the 1990s unearthed more carefully evaluated evidence of Gallo-Roman remains. A modern aerial survey detected fortification lines that might well be elements of the inner and outer siege walls that Caesar tells us he built to corral the Gauls.

Then there is the matter of the horse bones. The remains of three different breeds of horses have been found near the site. Does this prove the presence of Roman, Gaulish and Germanic (Roman mercenary) cavalries?

Battles are usually brief, chaotic events, and battlefield archaeology can add a level of precision and detail to the study of historic battles that few written accounts can offer. It can tell us about how the opposing armies used the terrain, how they deployed and adapted their tactics, and the "fog of war" – the chaos when command and control breaks down and an army's discipline starts to disintegrate.

Found in the 1980s near Rachet Hill at Entre-deux-Monts near Chaux-des-Crotenay, this iron spearhead is typical of the spears produced from the Gaulish era (La Tène) up to the Middle Ages.

What Lies Beneath

For archaeology, water was the final frontier. Deep-sea diving is the equivalent of entering an untamed universe, with its own ruthless rules. This is even true of relatively placid seas like the Mediterranean. Of the dive team assembled in 1901 to work at 112–164 ft (34–50 m) deep at Antikythera, two men were severely injured and another lost his life.

Trailblazer

There was a time when archaeologists had to rely entirely on divers for scraps of information. All this changed in the 1960s, when the "father" of this science, George Bass, realized it was far easier to train an archaeologist to dive than to train a diver to be an archaeologist.

Bass conducted the first truly scientific excavation of an ancient shipwreck, despite widespread scepticism from his colleagues. At the time, the *Gelidonya* wreck of the 2nd millennium BCE was the oldest ship ever found. To study, monitor and record it, Bass invented the underwater grid; a series of flexible telescopic poles, and he used early forms of metal detectors to locate artefacts. His groundbreaking work in Turkey included the famous *Uluburun* wreck, which provided a unique window into the Bronze Age world.

With the ability to investigate areas that were once "no-go", sites such as Shipwreck Alley in the deep waters of the Great Lakes, the scuppered flagship of the pirate Bluebeard or World War II aircraft graveyards relating to the Battle of Saipan submerged in the Pacific became accessible.

THE ANTIKYTHERA MECHANISM

In the early days of marine archaeology, undersea exploration was the preserve of skilled sponge divers. In 1900, diver Ilias Stadiatis emerged from the waves near the village of Antikythera holding the bronze arm of a submerged Greek statue. His discovery led to some truly extraordinary finds, including that of the Antikythera Mechanism. Dating from the 1st or 2nd century BCE, this truly remarkable navigation device proves that the ancient Greeks had highly sophisticated navigation techniques. One of today's biggest threats to underwater archaeology is trawler fishing, which destroys not only ocean life but all archaeological evidence on the sea bed. This is particularly problematic in the Mediterranean, and some archaeologists believe that discoveries like the Anthikythera device could never be made today.

The Dangers of the Deep

Even in the 1960s, the dangers were legion: nitrogen narcosis, being caught in underwater currents, or becoming disorientated in conditions of low visibility. Building on a century of effort by numerous inventors (many of whom died in the process), Jacques Cousteau and Emile Gagnan developed the Aqua-Lung in 1943, crucially improving the "demand-regulator" still used on SCUBA sets today.

Using remote-controlled robotic vehicles equipped with side-scan sonar and GPS, modern archaeologists can survey the sea floor systematically, using lighting rigs to illuminate the seabed and high definition video cameras that record and relay information in real time. Finds can be examined and recorded without bringing a single artefact up on to dry land.

Strangely enough, one of the biggest difficulties with marine archaeology is finding a site in the first place. The dive team Ocean Discovery searched for the 16th-century, Swedish warship *Mars* for years. They finally found it in 2011 in the Baltic sea east of Öland, immaculately preserved at a depth of 245 ft (75 m). One of the greatest shipwrecks discovered is the *Batavia*, a treasure ship of the Dutch East India Company that yielded some amazing finds, including jewellery.

The Ship of Dreams

On 15 April 1912, the RMS *Titanic* hit an iceberg on its maiden voyage to New York. Seventy-three years after the sinking, on 1 September 1985, an unmanned deep-sea vehicle disturbed the darkness of the ocean floor. Named after the mythical seafarer Jason's sleek and beautiful ship, the *Argo* was revolutionary; a hi-tech submersible towed at the end of miles of coaxial cable by the Woods

Hole Oceanographic Institution (WHOI) ship *Knorr*. Expedition leader Dr Robert Ballard had already tried and failed a number of times to locate *Titanic*, but now the *Argo* could send a stream of grainy images from the deep back to the ship.

Even then, Ballard only succeeded in locating the liner by changing his strategy; instead of searching for the ship itself, he looked for its debris field. At 2.00 am – almost the same time as *Titanic* went down – *Argo* stumbled upon the murky outline of a boiler, covered with "rivers of rust".

Technological Advancements

Titanic has since become an excavation of extraordinary "firsts". George Tulloch's metallurgical tests calibrated the levels of its disintegration, but his real interest was salvage. Miraculously, he recovered items such as intact letters, stowed in phantom passenger Howard Irwin's steamer trunk. Despite having a greatly sought-after and expensive ticket, Irwin had never actually boarded.

Inspired, James Cameron, the director of the film *Titanic*, and his team sent small robots deep into the bow that provided detailed information about the sinking and what remained. Progressively smaller and more agile bots were subsequently able to explore the wreck's hidden rooms and galleys. By 2010, an expedition led by James Delgado was able to create a comprehensive 3D map of the site and the surrounding debris field, using autonomous underwater vehicles (AUVs) and remotely operated vehicles (ROVs).

The technology developed for deep ocean archaeology is now immensely sophisticated. It includes collision avoidance software, proton magnetometers, high-resolution multi-beam profiling sonar, dual-frequency side-scan sonar, sub-bottom profiling sonar and conductivity, depth, and temperature sensors.

Submerged Cities

In addition to the numerous shipwrecks that have been investigated over the years, and continue to be, marine archaeologists are also searching for and examining the ruins of cities. In many cases, cities have disappeared into the sea due to the aftermath of seismic events.

Teams continue to investigate sites such as the port of Alexandria in Egypt or Port Royal in Jamaica. Baiae in Italy is another such site. It lies on a beautiful bay near the modern town of Bacoli, in the northeastern corner of the Bay of Naples. It was the private pleasure park of Rome's Augustan Age emperors. Nero killed his mother here, and the historian Seneca described it as a "harbour of vice". Volcanic activity caused half the town to sink beneath the waves and Baiae will take several decades to map and explore.

Bibliography

Alva, Walter & Donnan, Christopher B.: *Royal Tombs of Sipan*, Fowler Museum of Cultural History, Los Angeles, 1830

Atwood, Roger: *Stealing History: Tomb Raiders, Smugglers and the Looting of the Ancient World*, St Martin's Griffin, New York, 2006

Bahn, Paul: *The Complete Illustrated History of World Archaeology*, Lorenz Books, London, 2013

Beard, Mary: Pompeii: *The Life of a Roman Town*, Profile Books, London, 2010

Carver, Martin: *The Sutton Hoo Story: Encounters with Early England*, Boydell & Brewer, Woodbridge, 2017

Castleden, Rodney: *Minoan Life on Bronze Age Crete*, Routledge, London, 1993

Catling, Christopher: *A Practical Handbook of Archaeology: A Beginner's Guide to Unearthing The Past*, Hermes House, London, 2014

Ceram, C. W.: *Gods, Graves and Scholars: The Story of Archaeology*, Orion, London, 2001

Charles River Editors: "The Minoans and Myceneans: The Civilisations that first developed Ancient Greek Culture", 2016

Christie, Agatha: *Come, Tell Me How You Live: Memories from Archaeological Expeditions in the Mysterious Middle East*, HarperCollins, London, 2015 (Reissue)

Cline, Eric H.: *The Trojan War: A Very Short Introduction* (Very Short Introductions), Oxford University Press USA, New York, 2013

Dalley, Stephanie: *The Mystery of The Hanging Garden of Babylon: An Elusive Wonder Traced*, Oxford University Press, Oxford, 2015

Donnan, Christopher B.: *Royal Tombs of Sipan, University of California Press*, Oakland, 1995

Galaty, Michael L. & Watkinson, Charles (Eds): *Archaeology Under Dictatorship*, Springer US, New York, 2010

Gamble, Clive: *Archaeology: The Basics*, Routledge, London, 2015

Gere, Cathy: *The Tomb of Agamemnon: Mycenae and the Search for a Hero*, Profile Books, London, 2016

Hawass, Zawi: *The Valley of the Golden Mummies*, Abrams, New York, 2000

Hazel, John: *Who's Who in the Greek World*, Routledge, London, 2001

Hazel, John: *Who's Who in the Roman World*, Routledge, London, 2002

Joshel, Sandra & Petersen, Lauren Hackworth: *The Material Life of Roman Slaves*, Cambridge University Press, Cambridge, 2015

Kelley, Robert & Thomas, David: *Archaeology*, Wadsworth Publishing, Boston, 2016

Kirkpatrick, Sidney: *Lords of Sipan: A True Story of Pre-Inca Tombs, Archaeology, and Crime*, CreateSpace Independent Publishing, 2011

Leick, Gwendolyn: *Who's Who in the Ancient Near East*, Routledge, London, 2001

Maspero, G.: *Manual of Egyptian Archaeology*, Forgotten Books, London, 2017 (Classic reprint)

Mays, Simon: *The Archaeology of Human Bones*, Routledge, London, 2010

Miller, George L., Samford, Patricia, Shlasko, Ellen & Madsen, Andrew: "Telling Time for Archaeologists", Northeast Historical Archaeology, 2000 (Essay)

Morley, Neville: *Ancient History: Key Themes and Approaches*, Routledge, London, 1999

Pearson, Mike Parker & Pollard, Joshua: Stonehenge: *Making Sense of a Prehistoric Mystery* (Council for British Archaeology's Archaeology for All Series), Council for British Archaeology, London, 2015

Pollock, Susan: *Archaeologies of the Middle East: Critical Perspectives* (Wiley Blackwell Studies in Global Archaeology), John Wiley & Sons, London, 2004

Powers, Thomas: *The Killing of Crazy Horse*, Vintage Books, London, 2011

Preston, John: *The Dig*, Penguin, London, 2008 (plus press interview, *The Guardian*)

Renfrew, Colin (Ed.): *Archaeology: The Key Concepts* (Routledge Key Guides), Routledge, London, 2004

Renfrew, Colin & Bahn, Paul: *Archaeology: Theory, Methods and Practice*, Thames & Hudson, London, 2016

Rice, Michael: *Who's Who in Ancient Egypt*, Routledge, London, 2001

Schliemann, Heinrich: *Mycenae: A Narrative of researches and discoveries at Mycenae and Tiryns*, HardPress Publishing, USA, 2013

Thompson, Jason: *Wonderful Things: A History of Egyptology*, The American University in Cairo Press, Cairo, 1841

White, Tim D. & Folkens, Pieter A.: *The Human Bone Manual*, Academic Press, Oxford, 2005

Wilkinson, T. J.: *Archaeological Landscapes of the Near East*, University of Arizona Press, Tucson, 2003

Winckelmann, John & Lodge, G. Henry: *History of Ancient Art (Vols I & II)*, Wildside Press, Maryland, 2011

Woodward, Christopher: *In Ruins*, Vintage, London, 2002

Xiaoneng Yang, *New Perspectives on China's Past: Chinese Archaeology in the Twentieth Century*, Yale University Press, London, 2004

The author would like to acknowledge the research assistance of some journals, in particular: *Archaeology*, *Current Archaeology*, *National Geographic*, *Nature*, *New Scientist* and *The Smithsonian*.

Index

INDEX

INDEX

INDEX

INDEX

INDEX

Picture credits

Alamy: p.155 Alamy/David Warren, p.281 Alamy/Images & Stories.

Getty Images: p.20 Getty Images/ Paul D. Stewart, p.39 Getty Images/ De Agostini / G. Dagli Orti, p.79 Getty Images /CM Dixon/Print Collector.

Metropolitan Museum of Art: p.145 Metropolitan Museum of Art (Dodge Fund, 1933), p.151 Metropolitan Museum of Art (Munsy Fund, 1931), p.177 Metropolitan Museum of Art (The Elisha Whittelsey Collection, The Elisha Whittelsey Fund 1959).

Public domain: p.18, p.24, p.42, p.48, p.53, p.70, p.85, p.104, (top and bottom) p.108, p.119, p.124, p.129, p.138, p.174, p.188, p.199, p.200, p.213, p.215, p.220, p.230, p.233, p.237, p.239, p.241, p.262, p.278, p.284.

RMN France: p.7 Réunion des Musées Nationaux/ © Inrap, Dist. RMN-Grand Palais/Denis Gliksman.

Shutterstock.com: p.10, p.28, p.31, p.37, p.43, p.46, p.50, p.55, p.72, p.83, p.89, p.106, p.121, p.128, p.133, p.161, p.165, p.168, p.181, p.195, p.196, p.209, p.250, p.257, p.269.